Slimmers

BLOOMSBURY KITCHEN LIBRARY

Slimmers

Bloomsbury Books
London

This edition published 1995 by Bloomsbury Books,
an imprint of The Godfrey Cave Group,
42 Bloomsbury Street, London, WC1B 3QJ.

ISBN 1 85471 592 5

Printed and bound in Great Britain.

Contents

Celeriac in a Creamy Mustard Dressing

Serves 4

Working
(and total)
time: about
15 minutes

Calories
45
Protein
3g
Cholesterol
0mg
Total fat
2g
Saturated fat
1g
Sodium
30mg

2 tsp	golden mustard seeds	**2 tsp**	**1**	celeriac (about 500g/1lb),	**1**
½ tbsp	balsamic vinegar	**½ tbsp**		peeled and cut into thin julienne	
90 g	fromage frais	**3 oz**			

In a small, heavy frying pan, heat the mustard seeds for a few seconds, until they begin to pop. Transfer the mustard seeds to a small bowl; mix in the Dijon mustard, balsamic vinegar and *fromage frais* to make a creamy dressing.

Place the celeriac strips in a serving bowl and toss them with the mustard dressing until they are thoroughly coated. Either serve the salad immediately or place it in the refrigerator until serving time, stirring it well just before serving.

Grated Carrot Salad

Serves 4

Working
(and total)
time: about
10 minutes

Calories
30
Protein
2g
Cholesterol
0mg
Total fat
2g
Saturated fat
1g
Sodium
15mg

60 g	fromage frais	**2 oz**		**2 tsp**	tarragon leaves, chopped	**2 tsp**
1 tbsp	fresh lemon juice	**1 tbsp**		**250 g**	carrots, grated in a mouli	**8 oz**
½ tsp	grainy mustard	**½ tsp**			julienne or in a food processor	

In a small bowl, whisk together the *fromage frais*, lemon juice, mustard and tarragon leaves. Arrange the grated carrots in a large dish, spoon the dressing over them and serve the salad immediately.

Salad of Leaves and Flowers

Serves 6

Working (and total) time: about 10 minutes

Calories 75
Protein 1g
Cholesterol 0mg
Total fat 8g
Saturated fat 1g
Sodium 5mg

8	nasturtium leaves	**8**
2 tsp	lavender florets	**2 tsp**
1 tsp	borage flowers	**1 tsp**
2 tsp	thyme flowers	**2 tsp**
8	rose petals	**8**
6	violets or pansies	**6**
6	chervil sprigs	**6**

	Tarragon vinaigrette	
3 tbsp	safflower oil	**3 tbsp**
1½ tbsp	white wine vinegar	**1½ tbsp**
1 tsp	crushed coriander seeds	**1 tsp**
	freshly ground black pepper	
½ tsp	fresh tarragon leaves	**½ tsp**

In a small bowl, whisk together the oil and the vinegar for the dressing. Stir in the coriander seeds, some pepper and the tarragon, and mix well.

Lay the lettuce, the endive and the nasturtium leaves loosely in a deep bowl. Sprinkle the lavender, borage and thyme flowers, the rose petals, the violets or pansies and the chervil over the top. Add the dressing, toss the salad and serve it immediately.

Editor's Note: Any selection of mild and bitter salad leaves and edible flowers can be used. Aim for a combination that offers vivid contrasts of colour, flavour and texture. Perfect freshness of all ingredients is the sole requirement.

Middle-Eastern Spiced Carrot Salad

Serves 6

Working time: about 10 minutes

Total time: about 1 hour (includes cooling)

Calories 75
Protein 1g
Cholesterol 0mg
Total fat 5g
Saturated fat 1g
Sodium 190mg

1 kg	carrots, peeled and sliced into thick rounds	**2 lb**	
2	garlic cloves, sliced	**2**	
2 tbsp	virgin olive oil	**2 tbsp**	
¼ tsp	cayenne pepper	**¼ tsp**	
2 tsp	ground cumin	**2 tsp**	
2 tsp	fresh lemon juice	**2 tsp**	
¼ tsp	salt	**¼ tsp**	

Put the carrots and garlic into a saucepan. Cover them with hot water and boil them until they are soft—about 15 minutes. Drain the vegetables and mash them thoroughly.

In a small frying pan, heat the olive oil and fry the cayenne pepper and ground cumin for 1 minute. Stir the spice mixture into the carrot purée, mix in the lemon juice and the salt, and set the purée aside to cool at room temperature.

Minted Broccoli and Cauliflower

Serves 6

Working time:
about 15
minutes

Total time:
about 3 hours
and 15 minutes
(includes
marinating)

Calories
60
Protein
3g
Cholesterol
0mg
Total fat
5g
Saturated fat
1g
Sodium
10mg

350 g	trimmed cauliflower florets	**12 oz**	**½ tsp**	salt	**½ tsp**
250 g	trimmed broccoli florets	**8 oz**	**1 tbsp**	roughly cut chives	**1 tbsp**
6	sprigs fresh mint	**6**	**1 tbsp**	chopped fresh marjoram	**1 tbsp**
1 tbsp	white wine vinegar	**1 tbsp**	**1 tsp**	Dijon mustard	**1 tsp**
2	garlic cloves, crushed	**2**	**2 tbsp**	virgin olive oil	**2 tbsp**
				freshly ground black pepper	

Pour enough water into a large saucepan to fill it about 2.5 cm (1 inch) deep. Set a vegetable steamer in the pan and bring the water to the boil. Add the cauliflower and broccoli florets with four of the mint sprigs, and steam them, covered, until they are just tender— about 5 minutes. Pour the florets into a colander, refresh them under cold running water and drain them thoroughly. Discard the mint sprigs.

Put the vinegar, garlic, salt, marjoram, chives, mustard, olive oil and some black pepper in a large bowl and mix them well. Add the cauliflower and broccoli to the marinade, turning the florets gently until they are well coated. Cover the bowl with plastic film and allow the vegetables to marinate, in the refrigerator, for at least 3 hours.

Just before serving, garnish the vegetables with the leaves from the remaining mint sprigs.

Marinated Sardines

Serves 6

Working time: about 45 minutes

Total time: 2 to 3 days (includes marinating)

Calories 110

Protein 9g

Cholesterol 40mg

Total fat 8g

Saturated fat 2g

Sodium 105mg

600 g	fresh sardines, scaled, heads and tails removed and gutted, rinsed and patted dry	**1¼ lb**	
¾ tsp	salt	**¾ tsp**	
2	garlic cloves, chopped	**2**	
1 tbsp	chopped parsley	**1 tbsp**	
1 tbsp	virgin olive oil	**1 tbsp**	
12.5 cl	wine vinegar	**4 fl oz**	

Remove the backbone from each sardine and separate the two fillets lengthwise, leaving the skin intact.

Sprinkle the fish with the salt and place a layer of the fillets, skin side uppermost, in a shallow, non-reactive dish. Top the sardines wth the garlic and parsley. If the dish is not large enough to accommodate all the sardines in a single layer, add a second layer on top of the first.

Pour the oil and the vinegar over the fish, until the mixture covers the sardines. Cover the dish with plastic film and place it in the refrigerator to marinate for two to three days before serving.

Editor's Note: Fresh anchovies—small sprats, no longer than 12 cm (5 inches), can be used instead of sardines.

Asparagus with Tarragon Dressing

Serves 4

Working (and total) time: about 20 minutes

Calories 85

Protein 3g

Cholesterol 0mg

Total fat 8g

Saturated fat 1g

Sodium 100mg

500g	fresh asparagus, stalks trimmed and peeled to about 2.5 cm (1 inch) below the tips	**1lb**
1 tbsp	fresh lemon juice	**1 tbsp**
¼ tsp	salt	**¼ tsp**
	white pepper	
2 tbsp	virgin olive oil	**2 tbsp**
1 tbsp	chopped fresh tarragon	**1 tbsp**

To cook the asparagus, pour water into a large frying pan to a depth of 2.5 cm (1 inch), and bring the liquid to the boil. Line up the asparagus on the bottom of the pan, with all the tips facing in one direction. Position the pan so the thicker ends of the stalks lie over the centre of the heat source. Cook the asparagus until it is tender but still crisp—about 5 to 7 minutes.

While the spears are cooking, make the dressing. Mix the lemon juice, the salt and some white pepper in a small bowl. When the salt has dissolved, whisk in the olive oil.

With a fish slice, lift the asparagus gently out of the water, place it in a colander and refresh it briefly under cold running water. Drain the asparagus a second time and pat it dry with a clean tea towel. Arrange the spears on individual warmed dishes, spoon the dressing over them and sprinkle with the chopped tarragon.

Editor's Note: Peeling the asparagus ensures that the stalks cook at the same rate as the tender tips.

Steamed Cucumber with Herb and Yogurt Sauce

Serves 4

Working
(and total)
time: about
20 minutes

Calories
50
Protein
3g
Cholesterol
0mg
Total fat
3g
Saturated fat
2g
Sodium
40mg

1	large cucumber	1
	freshly ground black pepper	
250 g	thick Greek yogurt	8 oz
1 tbsp	chopped fresh dill	1 tbsp
1 tbsp	chopped parsley	1 tbsp
$\frac{1}{2}$ tbsp	chopped fresh tarragon	$\frac{1}{2}$ tbsp
4	fresh tarragon sprigs	4

With a sharp knife, peel the cucumber and chop it into 2.5 cm (1 inch) pieces. Remove the seeds from the centre of each piece with an apple corer. Pour enough water into a saucepan to fill it about 2.5 cm (1 inch) deep. Set a vegetable steamer in the pan and bring the water to the boil. Place the cucumber pieces in the steamer, season with some black pepper, cover the saucepan and steam until the cucumber is just heated through—3 to 4 minutes.

While the cucumber is steaming, prepare the sauce by mixing together the Greek yogurt, dill, parsley and chopped tarragon in a small saucepan. Heat the mixture over very low heat until the yogurt is warm, but not hot—about 1 minute.

Using a slotted spoon, transfer the cucumber pieces to warmed plates. Garnish the cucumber with the tarragon sprigs and serve with the warm yogurt sauce.

Mushrooms with Mussels

Serves 4

Working (and total) time about 35 minutes

Calories
90
Protein
11g
Cholesterol
30mg
Total fat
5g
Saturated fat
2g
Sodium
130mg

16	mussels, scrubbed and debearded	16
4	large cap mushrooms (about 175g/6 oz), wiped clean, stalks finely chopped, caps left whole	4
1 tbsp	finely chopped shallot	1 tbsp
12.5cl	dry white wine	4 fl oz
15g	unsalted butter, diced	$\frac{1}{2}$ oz
2 tbsp	torn basil leaves	2 tbsp
	freshly ground black pepper	
8	opal basil leaves (four large and four small)	8

Pour 4 tablespoons of water into a large saucepan. Add the mussels, cover the pan and bring the water to the boil. Steam the mussels until their shells open—4 to 5 minutes. Transfer the opened mussels to a shallow dish; discard any that remain closed.

Place the mushroom caps, dome side uppermost, on a piece of greaseproof paper and set them on the rack of a steamer or a colander placed over a saucepan of boiling water. Cover the mushrooms with a lid and steam them for 5 minutes; remove them from the heat and keep them warm.

Put the mushroom stalks and the shallots into a small saucepan, pour in the wine and simmer gently until the vegetables are tender—3 to 4 minutes. Increase the heat and boil until the liquid has reduced by half. Reduce the heat to very low and stir in the diced butter, piece by piece. Add the basil leaves, the mussels and some black pepper; keep the mixture warm over a low heat.

Place the large opal basil leaves on four plates and place a mushroom cap upside down on each one. Pile the mussel mixture into the mushrooms, top with a small opal basil leaf and serve hot.

Editor's Note: Opal basil is a red-leafed variety of basil with a lemony scent. If this is unobtainable, substitute lemon balm, oakleaf lettuce or other attractive salad leaves.

Plaice with Lemon and Parsley

Serves 8

Working (and total) time: about 30 minutes

Calories 65
Protein 11g
Cholesterol 35mg
Total fat 2g
Saturated fat 0g
Sodium 125mg

8	plaice fillets (125 g/4 oz each), skinned	**8**
⅛ tsp	salt	**⅛ tsp**
	freshly ground black pepper	
1	small onion, very finely chopped	**1**

2 tbsp	finely chopped parsley	**2 tbsp**
3 tbsp	fresh lemon juice	**3 tbsp**
4 tbsp	white wine	**4 tbsp**
8	thin lemon slices	**8**

Lay the fillets flat on a work surface, skinned side up. Season them with the salt and some pepper.

In the base of a shallow serving dish, spread out the onion and parsley, and sprinkle with the lemon juice and white wine. Double over each fillet, with the skinned side in, and arrange the fillets on top of the onion and parsley in two overlapping rows. Tuck the lemon slices between the fillets.

Cover the dish loosely with plastic film, then microwave on high until the fish is opaque—3 to 4 minutes. Rotate the dish once during the cooking time.

Let the fish stand, still covered with plastic film, for 3 minutes. Then remove the film and serve the plaice straight from the dish, spooning a little of the cooking liquid over each fillet.

Editor's Note: The fish and its cooking liquid may also be served cold, garnished with a salad of radicchio leaves.

Bacon-Stuffed Mushrooms

Serves 4

Working
(and total)
time: about
20 minutes

Calories
100
Protein
7g
Cholesterol
15mg
Total fat
6g
Saturated fat
2g
Sodium
500mg

4	large field mushrooms (300g/10 oz), rinsed, dried, stalks removed	4	100 g	lean unsmoked bacon rashers, trimmed of rind and all fat	3½ oz
1 tbsp	dry vermouth	**1 tbsp**	**1 tbsp**	virgin olive oil	**1 tbsp**
4 tbsp	coarsely chopped parsley	**4 tbsp**	**15 g**	fresh wholemeal breadcrumbs	½ oz
1	garlic clove, crushed	**1**		freshly ground black pepper	

Arrange the mushroom caps upside down in a single layer in a shallow dish, and sprinkle them with the dry vermouth and parsley. Cover the mushroom caps loosely with plastic film.

To make the stuffing, cut the bacon into small strips. Put the bacon and the crushed garlic in a bowl, stir in the olive oil, and microwave on high until the bacon begins to release its juices—about 1 minute. Stir the breadcrumbs and some pepper into the bacon mixture. Microwave the mixture on high until it is crisp—about 1 minute. Cover the stuffing with plastic film and keep it warm while you cook the mushrooms.

Leaving the mushrooms loosely covered, microwave them on high for 3 minutes, until they are just tender. Remove the plastic film, spread the bacon stuffing on top of the mushroom caps, and microwave on high until they are hot—about 30 seconds. Serve the stuffed mushrooms immediately.

Wilted Spinach Salad

Serves 4 as
a side dish

Working
time: about
15 minutes

Total time:
about 20
minutes

Calories
95
Protein
5g
Cholesterol
0mg
Total fat
1g
Saturated fat
0g
Sodium
200mg

6 tbsp	rice vinegar	**6 tbsp**
1 tbsp	sugar	**1 tbsp**
2 tsp	low-sodium soy sauce or shoyu	**2 tsp**
2 tsp	sweet chili sauce	**2 tsp**
2 tbsp	cornflour, mixed with 12.5 cl (4 fl oz) unsalted chicken stock	**2 tbsp**
125 g	pearl onions, peeled, blanched in boiling water for 2 minutes	**4 oz**
250 g	canned straw mushrooms, drained, stem tips cut off, or 300 g (10 oz) fresh mushrooms, wiped clean and stemmed	**8 oz**
500 g	fresh spinach, washed, stemmed, dried and torn into pieces	**1 lb**
1	sheet nori, crumbled (optional)	**1**

Combine all of the ingredients except the spinach and nori in a bowl. Stir the mixture well, then microwave it on high until it thickens slightly—about 3 minutes.

Thoroughly stir the dressing again, then pour it over the spinach. Toss the spinach to coat it evenly; sprinkle it with the nori if you are using it, and serve the salad at once.

Julienned Beetroots with Dijon Mustard

Serves 4 as a first course

Working time: about 15 minutes

Total time: about 30 minutes

Calories 70
Protein 1g
Cholesterol 0mg
Total fat 4g
Saturated fat 0g
Sodium 115mg

3	beetroots, of equal size (about 350 g/12 oz)	**3**
1	shallot, finely chopped	**1**
1½ tbsp	Dijon mustard	**1½ tbsp**
1tbsp	red wine vinegar	**1tbsp**
	freshly ground black pepper	
1 tbsp	virgin olive oil	**1 tbsp**
1	round lettuce (about 125 g/4 oz), washed and dried	**1**

Rinse the beetroots but do not pat them dry. Put them on a plate and microwave them on high for 6 to 8 minutes, turning them over about half way through the cooking time. Remove them from the oven, wrap them in a large piece of aluminium foil, and let them stand for 15 minutes to complete their cooking.

In a small bowl, combine the shallot, mustard, vinegar, some pepper and 1 tablespoon of water. Whisk in the oil and set the vinaigrette aside.

Peel and julienne the beetroots. Combine the julienne with about three quarters of the vinaigrette; toss well and refrigerate until cool.

Just before serving, slice the lettuce into chiffonade and toss it with the remaining vinaigrette. Divide the lettuce evenly among four salad plates, top with the beetroot julienne, and serve at once.

Scallop and Courgette Salad on a Bed of Radicchio

Serves 4 as
a main course
at lunch

Working time:
about 15
minutes

Total time:
about 40
minutes

Calories
120
Protein
15g
Cholesterol
30mg
Total fat
4g
Saturated fat
1g
Sodium
210mg

350 g	scallops, rinsed, the bright white connective tissue removed	**12 oz**
1	small courgette (125 g/4 oz), trimmed and cut into paper-thin slices	**1**
2 tbsp	thinly sliced crystallized ginger	**2 tbsp**
2 ½ tbsp	fresh lemon juice	**2 ½ tbsp**
¼ tsp	salt	**¼ tsp**
	freshly ground black pepper	
1 tbsp	virgin olive oil	**1 tbsp**
1	head of radicchio or red-leaf lettuce (about 125 g/4 oz), washed, dried and cut into chiffonade	**1**

Slice the scallops into very thin rounds. In a shallow glass bowl, combine the scallops with the courgette, 1½ tablespoons of the ginger, 1½ tablespoons of the lemon juice, the salt and some pepper. Set the bowl aside for 5 minutes; stir the contents and allow them to stand for 5 minutes more.

Microwave the scallops and courgette in their marinade for 2 to 3 minutes on high, stirring midway through the cooking.

Put the remaining ½ tablespoon of ginger in a small bowl. Set a strainer over the bowl and pour the scallop mixture into the strainer. Refrigerate both strainer and bowl for at least 15 minutes.

At the end of the chilling time, whisk the remaining tablespoon of lemon juice, the oil and more pepper into the marinade; then stir in the scallop mixture. Arrange the chiffonade in the shape of a wreath on a plate. Mound the salad in the centre and serve at once.

Clam and Sweetcorn Salad

Serves 6 as
a main course
at lunch

Working time:
about 45
minutes

Total time:
about 1 hour
and 15
minutes

Calories
150

Protein
9g

Cholesterol
25mg

Total fat
8g

Saturated fat
1g

Sodium
100mg

5	spring onions, finely chopped	5
1	garlic clove, finely chopped	1
¼ litre	dry white wine	8 fl oz
4 tbsp	fresh lemon juice	4 tbsp
36	small hard-shell clams, scrubbed	36
250 g	mushrooms, wiped clean, stemmed and quartered	8 oz
3	carrots, sliced thinly	3
3	sticks celery, sliced thinly	3
325 g	fresh sweetcorn kernels	11 oz
1 tbsp	chopped parsley	1 tbsp
1 tbsp	white wine vinegar	1 tbsp
	freshly ground black pepper	
2 tbsp	virgin olive oil	2 tbsp
500 g	fresh spinach, washed, stemmed and cut into chiffonade	1 lb

Combine the spring onions, garlic, wine and lemon juice in a large pan. Bring to the boil. Add the clams to the boiling liquid. Cover and cook the clams until they open—3 minutes. Lift the clams into a large bowl; discard any that remain closed. Strain the broth through muslin into a bowl.

When the clams are cool, remove them from their shells. Rinse each clam in the broth. Transfer to a bowl; cover and refrigerate.

Strain the broth and pour into the saucepan. Add the mushrooms and remaining lemon juice. Bring to the boil, then cover and simmer for 2 minutes. Lift the mushrooms into a bowl.

Add the carrots and celery to the clam broth; cover and simmer for 3 minutes. Add the carrots and celery to the mushrooms; do not discard broth. Let the vegetables cool.

Set a steamer in the saucepan and put in the sweetcorn. Bring to the boil, tightly cover, and steam for 3 minutes.

Whisk the parsley, vinegar, some pepper and the oil into the broth to make a dressing. Add all the vegetables to the clams; pour half of the dressing onto the salad and toss it well.

Arrange the salad with spinach on separate plates.

Mussel and Sprouted Lentil Salad

Serves 6 as a
main course
at lunch

Working time:
about 35
minutes

Total time:
about 1 hour
(includes
chilling)

Calories
120
Protein
9g
Cholesterol
25mg
Total fat
4g
Saturated fat
0g
Sodium
225mg

36	mussels, scrubbed and debearded	**36**
2	carrots, julienned	**2**
¼ tsp	salt	**¼ tsp**
	freshly ground black pepper	
2 tbsp	white wine vinegar	**2 tbsp**
1 tbsp	safflower oil	**1 tbsp**

1	garlic clove, finely chopped	**1**
500 g	ripe tomatoes, skinned, seeded, coarsely chopped,	**1 lb**
1 tbsp	fennel seeds	**1 tbsp**
150 g	sprouted lentils	**5 oz**
1	lettuce, washed and dried	**1**

Bring 12.5 cl (4 fl oz) of water to the boil in a large pan; add the mussels and cover the pan. Steam the mussels until they open—about 3 minutes. Lift out the mussels and set them aside; discard any that remain closed. Strain the cooking liquid through doubled muslin. Reserve the liquid.

When the mussels are cool, remove them from their shells. Dip each mussel into the reserved liquid to rinse away any residual sand. Put the rinsed mussels into a large bowl. Strain the liquid again and set aside.

Bring 1.5 litres (2 ½ pints) of water to the boil in a saucepan. Add the carrots and blanch them for 2 minutes, then refresh under cold water. Drain well, add them to the

mussels, and season with the salt, some pepper and the vinegar.

Heat the oil in a heavy-bottomed saucepan over medium heat; add the garlic and sauté it for 1 minute. Add the tomatoes, fennel seeds and 12.5 cl (4 fl oz) of the mussel liquid; bring the liquid to the boil. Reduce to a strong simmer and cook until nearly all the liquid has evaporated—about 5 minutes.

Meanwhile, blanch the lentil sprouts in boiling water for 3 minutes. Drain them, refresh them and drain them again. Add the sprouts and the tomato mixture to the mussels and toss well. Refrigerate the salad for 1 hour before presenting it on a bed of lettuce.

Turkey Salad with Green and Red Grapes

<table>
<tr><td>Serves 4 as
a main course</td></tr>
<tr><td>Working time:
about 20
minutes</td></tr>
<tr><td>Total time:
about 1 hour
and 30
minutes</td></tr>
</table>

Calories
290

Protein
27g

Cholesterol
60mg

Total fat
17g

Saturated fat
2g

Sodium
200mg

500 g	skinless turkey breast meat	**1 lb**
2 tbsp	fresh lemon juice	**2 tbsp**
1 tbsp	virgin olive oil	**1 tbsp**
1 tbsp	fresh thyme, or 1 tsp dried thyme	**1 tbsp**
⅛ tsp	salt	**⅛ tsp**
	freshly ground black pepper	
2 tbsp	sliced almonds	**2 tbsp**

80 g	seedless green grapes	**2½ oz**
80 g	seedless red grapes	**2½ oz**
3	spring onions, trimmed and thinly sliced	**3**
4 tbsp	vinaigrette	**4 tbsp**
1	small red-leaf lettuce, washed and dried	**1**

Preheat the oven to 190°C (375°F or Mark 5). Put the turkey meat in a small baking dish and sprinkle it with the lemon juice, oil, thyme, salt and some pepper. Rub the seasonings into the meat and let it marinate at room temperature for 20 minutes.

At the end of the marinating time, roast the meat, turning it once, until it feels firm but springy to the touch—about 20 minutes.

While the meat is cooking, spread the almonds on a small baking sheet and toast them in the oven until they are golden-brown—about 4 minutes. Set the toasted almonds aside.

When the turkey has finished cooking, remove it from the oven and let it cool in the dish. As soon as the meat is cool enough to handle, remove it from the dish and cut it diagonally into thin slices. Lay the slices in the pan juices and refrigerate them for at least 30 minutes.

To assemble the salad, combine the grapes, spring onions and vinaigrette in a bowl. Arrange the turkey slices on the lettuce leaves and mound the grapes and spring onions on top; sprinkle the salad with the toasted almonds and serve immediately.

Squid Salad with Spring Onions and Coriander

Serves 4 as a main course

Working time: about 25 minutes

Total time: about 1 hour

Calories **175**
Protein **16g**
Cholesterol **223mg**
Total fat **8g**
Saturated fat **1g**
Sodium **400mg**

600 g	small squid, cleaned and skinned, tentacles reserved	**1¼ lb**
2 tbsp	virgin olive oil	**2 tbsp**
¼ tsp	salt	**¼ tsp**
	freshly ground black pepper	
1 tsp	coriander seeds, crushed	**1 tsp**
2 tbsp	sherry vinegar	**2 tbsp**
1 tbsp	fresh lemon juice	**1 tbsp**
½	sweet red pepper, seeded, deribbed and diced	**½**
½	sweet yellow pepper, seeded, deribbed and diced	**½**
4	spring onions, trimmed and sliced diagonally into thin ovals	**4**
1	large round lettuce, washed, dried lemon slices for garnish	**1**

Slice the squid pouches into thin rings. Heat 1 tablespoon of the olive oil in a large, heavy frying pan over high heat. When the oil is hot, add the squid rings and tentacles, ⅛ teaspoon of the salt and some pepper. Sauté the squid, stirring constantly, until it turns opaque—about 2 minutes. Drain the squid well, reserving the cooking juices, and transfer the squid pieces to a large bowl; put the bowl in the refrigerator.

Pour the cooking juices into a small saucepan; add the crushed coriander and boil the liquid until only 2 tablespoons remain—about 3 minutes. Remove from the heat, then whisk in the vinegar, lemon juice, remaining salt and remaining oil. Pour this dressing over the squid; add the peppers and spring onions, and toss. Chill the salad for at least 30 minutes.

Just before serving the salad, grind in a generous amount of black pepper and toss well. Present the salad on the lettuce leaves, garnished with lemon slices.

Prawn Salad on Fresh Pineapple-Mango Relish

Serves 8 as
a main course
at lunch

Working time:
about 30
minutes

Total time:
about 1 hour

Calories
160
Protein
13g
Cholesterol
105mg
Total fat
4g
Saturated fat
1g
Sodium
200mg

2	large ripe mangoes	2
1	pineapple, peeled and cut into 5 mm (¼ inch) cubes	1
4 tbsp	fresh lime juice	4 tbsp
30 g	fresh coriander, finely chopped	1 oz
2	sweet red peppers, halved, seeded and deribbed	2
4 tbsp	mayonnaise	4 tbsp

750 g	cooked prawns, peeled, and deveined if necessary	1½ lb
4	spring onions, trimmed and thinly sliced	4
2 tbsp	very finely chopped fresh ginger root	2 tbsp
½ tsp	salt	½ tsp
1	fresh coriander sprig for garnish	1

To prepare the relish, first peel the mangoes and remove the flesh in pieces. Purée one quarter of the flesh in a food processor or a blender, then pass it through a sieve set over a bowl. Refrigerate the purée. Cut the remaining mango pieces into 5 mm (¼ inch) cubes and place them in a bowl. Add the pineapple, lime juice and chopped coriander; stir the relish and refrigerate it.

Dice one of the pepper halves and put the dice in a bowl with the prawns. Julienne the remaining pepper halves and set the julienne aside. Stir the mayonnaise, mango purée, spring onions, ginger and salt into the prawn-and-pepper mixture. Chill the salad in the refrigerator for at least 30 minutes.

To serve, spoon some of the pineapple-mango relish on to a large platter and surround it with some of the prawn salad. Top the relish with the remaining prawn salad; garnish the dish with the pepper julienne and the coriander sprig.

Monkfish, Broad Bean and Red Cabbage Salad

Serves 4 as
a main course

Working time:
about 20
minutes

Total time:
about 1 hour
(includes
chilling)

Calories
240
Protein
25g
Cholesterol
40mg
Total fat
6g
Saturated fat
0g
Sodium
365mg

500 g	monkfish fillet, trimmed, rinsed, dried	**1 lb**
¼ tsp	salt	**¼ tsp**
¼ tsp	white pepper	**¼ tsp**
300 g	fresh shelled broad beans, or frozen baby broad beans, thawed	**10 oz**
90 g	red cabbage, thinly sliced	**3 oz**
2 tbsp	chopped fresh mint, or 2 tsp dried mint	**2 tbsp**
3 tbsp	fish stock or unsalted chicken stock	**3 tbsp**
2 tbsp	sherry vinegar	**2 tbsp**
1 tbsp	safflower oil	**1 tbsp**
1 tbsp	chopped parsley	**1 tbsp**
1	lettuce, washed and dried	**1**

Cut the monkfish fillet crosswise into thin slices. Season the slices with the salt and some pepper.

Pour enough water into a saucepan to fill it about 2.5 cm (1 inch) deep. Set a vegetable steamer in the pan and bring the water to the boil. Put the monkfish slices into the steamer, tightly cover the pan, and steam the fish until it is opaque and firm to the touch—2 to 3 minutes. Transfer the monkfish slices to a large, shallow dish.

If you are using fresh broad beans, cook them in 1 litre (1¾ pints) of boiling water until they are barely tender—8 to 10 minutes—

then drain them and add them to the monkfish. (Frozen beans require only brief blanching.) Blanch the cabbage in 1 litre (1¾ pints) of boiling water for 3 minutes; drain the cabbage and add it to the monkfish and beans.

To prepare the dressing, whisk together the mint, stock, vinegar and oil. Pour the dressing over the contents of the dish; mix the ingredients thoroughly, then refrigerate the salad for 30 minutes.

Add the parsley to the salad and toss. Serve the salad on a bed of lettuce.

Shredded Beef Salad with Marinated Carrot Strips

Serves 8 as
a main course

Working time:
about 45
minutes

Total time:
about 4 hours

Calories
255

Protein
27g

Cholesterol
75mg

Total fat
12g

Saturated fat
4g

Sodium
190mg

3 tbsp	safflower oil	**3 tbsp**
1 kg	braising steak, trimmed of fat	**2 lb**
6	medium carrots	**6**
¼ litre	unsalted veal or chicken stock	**8 fl oz**
2	onions, coarsely chopped	**2**
3	garlic cloves, crushed	**3**
1 tbsp	fresh thyme, or 1 tsp dried thyme	**1 tbsp**
3	bay leaves	**3**
1 tsp	sugar	**1 tsp**
12.5 cl	cider vinegar	**4 floz**
¼ tsp	salt	**¼ tsp**
2 tbsp	hoisin sauce	**2 tbsp**
	freshly ground black pepper	
	several Chinese cabbage leaves	
4	spring onions	**4**

Sear the beef until well browned in 1 tablespoon of oil.

Slice one carrot thinly and add it to the pan with the stock, onions, garlic, thyme and bay leaves. Add water to a depth of 2.5 cm (1 inch). Cook the beef slowly until tender—about 3 hours. Add water as necessary.

Meanwhile pare long, thin strips from the remaining carrots; discard the cores. Mix with the sugar and all but 2 tablespoons of the vinegar; toss well. Marinate, stirring occasionally.

Remove the cooked beef from the pan. Strain the cooking liquid; pour half into a small pan and discard the rest. Rapidly boil

until only 4 tablespoons remain. Skim fat off and set aside.

Heat 1 tablespoon of oil in the pan. Add the beef and salt; sauté, stirring for 1 minute. Add the reduced cooking liquid, remaining vinegar and hoisin sauce; Season with pepper and cook 1 minute more. Chill the beef.

Clean the sauté pan, then return it to the stove. Cook the carrot strips and their marinade. Sauté, stirring in the remaining oil until all the liquid has evaporated. Chill for 30 minutes.

Arrange the carrot strips and beef on the chinese cabbage, garnished with spring onion.

Spinach and Chinese Cabbage Pie

Serves 6

Working time: about 30 minutes

Total time: about 1 hour and 20 minutes

Calories 170
Protein 12g
Cholesterol 90mg
Total fat 10g
Saturated fat 5g
Sodium 430mg

500 g	Chinese cabbage, leaves separated and washed	**1 lb**
500 g	spinach, washed, stems removed	**1 lb**
2	eggs	**2**
1	egg white	**1**
175 g	low-fat cottage cheese	**6 oz**
3 tbsp	cut chives	**3 tbsp**
2 tbsp	chopped fresh marjoram	**2 tbsp**
¼ tsp	salt	**¼ tsp**
	freshly ground black pepper	
6	sheets phyllo pastry, each about 45 by 30 cm (18 by 12 inches)	**6**
45 g	unsalted butter, melted	**1½ oz**

Bring a large saucepan of water to the boil, add the Chinese cabbage and cook for 1 minute, until wilted. Using a slotted spoon, lift the leaves out of the water into a colander and drain them well. Blanch the spinach in the same water for 1 minute, then pour into a colander and refresh under cold water. Squeeze the spinach dry in muslin. Roughly chop the Chinese cabbage and the spinach.

Put the eggs and egg white into a large mixing bowl and whisk them lightly together. Add the Chinese cabbage and spinach, the cottage cheese, chives, marjoram, salt and some black pepper. Mix together. Set the bowl aside.

Preheat the oven to 190°C (375°F or Mark 5). Grease a 30 by 22 cm (12 by 9 inch) ovenproof dish.

Cut the sheets of phyllo pastry in half crosswise. Place one piece in the bottom of the prepared dish and brush it with a little of the melted butter. Add another three pieces, brushing each with melted butter. Pour the cabbage and spinach mixture into the dish and level the surface. Cover with the remaining eight pieces of phyllo, brushing each piece with melted butter. Mark the top with a diamond pattern.

Bake it for 50 to 55 minutes, until golden-brown.

Vegetable Lasagne

Serves 6

Working time:
about 1 hour
and 30
minutes

Total time:
about 2 hours
and 15
minutes

Calories
295
Protein
13g
Cholesterol
55mg
Total fat
12g
Saturated fat
5g
Sodium
280mg

18	sheets 'no pre-cook' lasagne	**18**
1 tbsp	virgin olive oil	**1 tbsp**
1	onion, finely chopped	**1**
1	leek, trimmed and sliced	**1**
2	garlic cloves, crushed	**2**
175 g	broccoli florets	**6 oz**
125 g	French beans, topped and tailed, cut into short lengths	**4 oz**
6	sticks celery, sliced	**6**
1	yellow pepper, sliced	**1**
1 tsp	mixed dried herbs	**1 tsp**
1 tbsp	chopped parsley	**1 tbsp**

400 g	canned tomatoes, sieved	**14 oz**
¼ tsp	salt	**¼ tsp**
	freshly groung black pepper	
30 g	Parmesan cheese	**1 oz**
	Nutmeg Sauce	
30 g	unsalted butter	**1 oz**
30 g	plain flour	**1 oz**
30 cl	skimmed milk	**pint**
½ tsp	freshly grated nutmeg	**½ tsp**
⅛ tsp	salt	**⅛ tsp**
	freshly ground black pepper	

Sauté the onion and leek in the oil until softened. Stir in the garlic, all the vegetables and herbs, the tomatoes and seasoning. Boil, the simmer, partially covered, until the vegetables are tender and the liquid has thickened.

Preheat the oven to 200°C (400°F or Mark 6).

Grease a large ovenproof dish and line the bottom with six sheets of lasagne. Pour in half of the vegetable filling then cover with six more sheets. Pour in the rest of the vegetables and place the remaining sheets on top.

To make the sauce, melt the butter in a saucepan over medium heat. Add the flour, then stir in the milk. Bring to the boil, stirring until it thickens. Stir in the nutmeg and seasoning. reduce the heat to low and simmer for 5 minutes, stirring frequently. Pour the sauce over the top and spread it to cover the entire surface. Sprinkle the Parmesan over the sauce. Cook in the oven for 40 minutes, until golden-brown and bubbling hot. ·

Spinach and Lamb Strudel

Serves 4

Working time: about 30 minutes

Total time: about 1 hour and 15 minutes

Calories 200
Protein 23g
Cholesterol 70mg
Total fat 7g
Saturated fat 3g
Sodium 235mg

300 g	lean lamb (from the leg or loin), trimmed of fat and finely diced	**10 oz**
250 g	fresh spinach, washed and stemmed	**8 oz**
250 g	button mushrooms, finely chopped	**8 oz**
1	onion, finely chopped	**1**
30 g	wholemeal breadcrumbs	**1 oz**

2	garlic cloves, crushed	**2**
¼ tsp	salt	**¼ tsp**
	freshly ground black pepper	**2**
2	sheets phyllo pastry, each 45 by 30 cm (18 by 12 inches)	
½ tsp	safflower oil	**½ tsp**
1 tsp	sesame seeds	**1 tsp**
	cherry tomatoes for garnish	

Preheat the oven to 190°C (375°F or Mark 5).

Set aside four spinach leaves for garnish then plunge the rest into a saucepan of boiling water, bring it back to the boil and cook for 1 minute. Drain it in a colander and rinse under cold water, then squeeze it dry and chop it finely.

Brush a non-stick frying pan with oil, heat it over a high heat then sear the lamb quickly. Remove the pan from the heat and stir in the spinach, mushrooms, onion, breadcrumbs, garlic, salt and pepper. Mix all the ingredients thoroughly together.

Lay one sheet of the phyllo on a work surface and cover it with the second sheet. Spoon the lamb filling along one short side of the phyllo, keeping it 2.5 cm (1 inch) away from the edge. Shape the filling into a firm sausage with your fingers. Roll up the strudel and transfer it to a baking sheet, seam side down. Squeeze the ends of the phyllo together lightly to stop the filling falling out. Brush the strudel with the oil and sprinkle it with the sesame seeds. Bake it until the pastry is golden—about 40 minutes. Leave it to cool for about 5 minutes before cutting it into eight slices. Serve the strudel garnished with the reserved spinach leaves and cherry tomatoes.

Lamb with Asparagus and Jerusalem Artichokes

Serves 6

Working time:
about 1 hour

Total time:
about 2 hours
and 30
minutes

Calories
225

Protein
30g

Cholesterol
80mg

Total fat
9g

Saturated fat
4g

Sodium
270mg

750 g	lean lamb	**1½ lb**
	cut into 7.5 cm (3 inch) strips	
500 g	asparagus, trimmed and peeled	**1 lb**
1 tsp	salt	**1 tsp**
½ tbsp	safflower oil	**½ tbsp**
3	shallots, halved	**3**

500 g	Jerusalem artichokes	**1 lb**
4 tsp	fresh lemon juice	**4 tsp**
60 g	watercress, blanched and chopped	**2 oz**
¼ tsp	white pepper	**¼ tsp**
3 tbsp	thick Greek yogurt	**3 tbsp**

Cut off the tips of the asparagus spears and set aside. Cook the stems in boiling water to cover, with ½ teaspoon of the salt, until they are soft—15 minutes. Lift them out, drain and set aside; strain and reserve the cooking liquid.

Heat the oil in a frying pan, and soften the shallots over a medium heat—5 minutes. Transfer to a fireproof casserole. Increase the heat under the frying pan and lightly brown the lamb strips then transfer them to the casserole. Pour the asparagus cooking liquid over the meat and shallots. Add water to the lamb. Simmer until the meat is tender—about 1 hour.

Meanwhile, put 1 teaspoon of the lemon juice into a non-reactive pan with 1 litre (1¾ pints) of water. Peel and chop the artichokes,

dropping them into the water immediately. Bring to the boil and cook the artichokes until tender—20 to 30 minutes. Drain the artichokes and purée them. Purée and sieve the asparagus stems. Set aside.

Skim off any fat from the casserole and remove the meat and shallots. Bring the liquid to the boil, add the asparagus tips and cook gently until tender—5 minutes. Lift out the tips and keep them warm.

Stir the purées and the watercress into the cooking liquid to make a sauce. Gently heat the sauce and season with lemon juice, salt and white pepper. Add the meat to the sauce and heat gently. Add the asparagus tips and swirl the yogurt on the top. Serve at once.

Saffron Chicken with Yogurt

Serves 6

Working time: about 30 minutes

Total time: about 1 day

Calories 210
Protein 28g
Cholesterol 90mg
Total fat 9g
Saturated fat 2g
Sodium 185mg

6	whole chicken legs, skinned	**6**
4 tbsp	unsalted chicken stock	**4 tbsp**
⅛ tsp	saffron (about 20 threads)	**⅛ tsp**
¼ tsp	salt	**¼ tsp**
	freshly ground black pepper	
12.5 cl	plain low-fat yogurt	**4 fl oz**

90 g	onion, chopped	**3 oz**
2	garlic cloves, finely chopped	**2**
1 tsp	grated fresh ginger root	**1 tsp**
4 tbsp	fresh lemon juice	**4 tbsp**
⅛ tsp	cayenne pepper	**⅛ tsp**
¼ tsp	ground cumin	**¼ tsp**

Combine the stock and saffron in a small saucepan over medium heat and bring them to a simmer. Remove the pan from the heat and let the saffron steep for about 5 minutes. The stock will turn golden.

Sprinkle the chicken legs with the salt and pepper. Put them in a shallow baking dish and dribble the stock and saffron mixture over them. Turn the legs to coat both sides and arrange them so that they do not touch.

Combine the yogurt, onion, garlic, ginger, lemon juice, cayenne pepper and cumin in a food processor or blender, and purée until smooth. Pour the mixture over the chicken legs and cover the dish with a sheet of plastic film. Refrigerate it for 8 hours or overnight. Preheat the grill. Remove the legs from the marinade and arrange them top side down in a foil-lined grill pan. Reserve the marinade. Position the grill pan 8 to 10 cm (3½ to 4 inches) below the heat source. Grill the legs for about 8 minutes on each side, basting them with the marinade every 2 minutes. The chicken is done when the juices run clear from a thigh pierced with the tip of a sharp knife.

Dressed Crab with Prawn and Yogurt Sauce

Serves 4

Working (and total) time: about 1 hour

Calories 230

Protein 25g

Cholesterol 100mg

Total fat 11g

Saturated fat 3g

Sodium 455mg

2	cooked crabs (1 kg/2 $\frac{1}{2}$ lb each)	**2**
	Prawn and yogurt sauce	
15 g	fresh ginger root, peeled	$\frac{1}{2}$ **oz**
175 g	peeled cooked prawns	**6 oz**
15 cl	plain yogurt	**5 fl oz**
1 tbsp	lemon juice	**1 tbsp**
$\frac{1}{4}$**tsp**	salt	$\frac{1}{4}$ **tsp**
	freshly ground black pepper	
1 tbsp	chopped chives	**1 tbsp**
	Garnish	
2 tbsp	chopped chives	**2 tbsp**
$\frac{1}{2}$ **tsp**	paprika	$\frac{1}{2}$ **tsp**
	lettuce leaves	
	lemon slices or wedges	

Prepare the crabs keeping the white and brown meats separate.

Neaten the empty crab shells by breaking away the thin part of the shell on the underside, following the natural curved line. Wash the shells thoroughly and dry well.

Fill the crab shells with the crab meat, placing the white meat to the sides, and the brown meat down the centre. Garnish with neat lines of chopped chives and paprika. Refrigerate while making the sauce.

To make the sauce, chop the ginger very finely. Put a few peeled prawns aside for garnish and roughly chop the rest. Blend the yogurt with the lemon juice, salt, pepper and 1 tablespoon of chopped chives, then stir in the ginger and prawns. Spoon the sauce into a serving bowl. Garnish it with a light sprinkling of chives, paprika and the reserved prawns.

Line a serving dish with lettuce leaves, place the crab shells on the dish, then garnish with the lemon slices. Serve the crabs accompanied by the sauce.

Ragout of Scallops and Red Peppers

Serves 4

Working
(and total)
time: about
45 minutes

Calories
225
Protein
21g
Cholesterol
40mg
Total fat
8g
Saturated fat
1g
Sodium
250mg

500 g	shelled scallops, bright white connective tissue removed	**1 lb**
2	sweet red peppers freshly ground black pepper	**2**
1 tbsp	fresh lime juice	**1 tbsp**
2 tbsp	red wine vinegar	**2 tbsp**
2 tsp	fresh thyme, or $\frac{1}{2}$ tsp dried thyme	**2 tsp**
2 tbsp	virgin olive oil	**2 tbsp**
250 g	mushrooms, wiped clean and quartered	**8 oz**
$\frac{1}{4}$ tsp	salt	**$\frac{1}{4}$ tsp**
12.5 cl	dry white wine	**4 fl oz**
1	bunch spring onions, trimmed and cut into 2.5 cm (1 inch) pieces	**1**
150 g	chicory, cut into 2.5 cm (1 inch) pieces, pieces separated	**5 oz**

Grill the peppers until blackened all over—about 15 minutes.

Meanwhile, rinse the scallops under cold water. Cut the larger scallops in half. Put the scallops in a bowl and sprinkle with black pepper. Stir in the lime juice and set.

Put the peppers in a bowl and cover with plastic film for 2 minutes. Working over the bowl to catch their juices, peel and seed the peppers. Coarsely chop the peppers and put them in a blender with their juices, the vinegar, thyme and some pepper; purée the mixture.

Heat the oil in a large, frying pan over medium-high. Add the mushrooms and sauté for 3 minutes, stirring once. Sprinkle the mushrooms with $\frac{1}{8}$ teaspoon of salt, then pour in the wine. Continue cooking, stirring occasionally, until almost all of the liquid has evaporated—3 to 5 minutes.

Pour the pepper purée into the frying pan. Place the scallops on top and sprinkle with more black pepper and the remaining salt. Cook for 1 minute, stirring. Add the spring onions and chicory and cook, stirring frequently, until the scallops are firm—2 to 3 minutes more. Serve immediately.

Squid Stewed in Red Wine

750 g	squid, cleaned and skinned	**1½ lb**
2 tbsp	virgin olive oil	**2 tbsp**
¼ tsp	salt	**¼ tsp**
20	garlic cloves	**20**
500 g	ripe tomatoes, skinned, seeded and chopped, or 400 g (14 oz) canned whole tomatoes, drained and chopped	**1 lb**

35 cl	red wine	**12 fl oz**
3	medium leeks, trimmed, split, washed thoroughly to remove all traces of grit, and chopped	**3**
250 g	courgettes, sliced into thin rounds	**8 oz**
4 tbsp	basil or flat parsley leaves, cut into thin strips	**4 tbsp**
	freshly ground black pepper	

Heat ½ tablespoon of the olive oil in a large, heavy frying pan over medium-high heat. Add the squid and sauté, stirring often, until opaque—2 to 3 minutes. Sprinkle ⅛ teaspoon of the salt on the squid and transfer to a large, fireproof casserole.

Reduce the heat under the frying pan to medium low. Pour 1 tablespoon of oil into the pan, then add the leeks and garlic cloves. Cover and cook, shaking the pan occasionally, until the leeks begin to turn golden-brown— about 10 minutes.

Transfer the leeks and garlic to the casserole containing the squid. Add the tomatoes and wine, and bring to the boil. Reduce the heat, cover and simmer the stew until the squid is tender—about 1 hour.

Meanwhile, pour the remaining oil into the frying pan over medium heat. Add the courgettes and cook, stirring occasionally, until the courgettes are soft but not brown—3 minutes. Sprinkle the courgettes with the remaining salt, transfer to a bowl and set aside.

Before serving the stew, add the softened courgettes, the basil or parsley, and some pepper; stir gently and serve immediately.

Red Mullet Marinated in Passion Fruit Juice

Serves 4

Working time:
about 25
minutes

Total time:
about 1 hour
and 10
minutes

Calories
270
Protein
39g
Cholesterol
75mg
Total fat
12g
Saturated fat
1g
Sodium
350mg

4	red mullet (about 250 g/8 oz each)	4	2 tsp	mixed dried herbs	2 tsp
8	large fresh or vacuum-packed vine leaves	8	½ tsp	salt	½ tsp
	Marinade			freshly ground black pepper	
3	passion fruit	3		**Garnish**	
1 tbsp	olive oil	1 tbsp		black olives	
				lemon wedges	

Remove the fins and scales from the mullet, slit each fish along the belly and remove the viscera. Rinse the fish under cold water and pat them dry with paper towels.

To prepare the marinade, cut the passion fruit in half and scoop out the flesh into a small nylon sieve. Place the sieve over a bowl and extract the juice from the flesh with the back of a spoon. Add the oil, herbs, salt and pepper to the passion fruit juice and mix thoroughly. Transfer the marinade to a shallow dish. Place the mullet in the dish, then turn them in the marinade until well coated. Cover and marinate the fish for 1 hour.

Remove the mullet from the marinade and wrap each fish in two vine leaves. Place them in a shallow dish, then brush them with the remaining marinade. Cover the dish loosely with plastic film.

Microwave the mullet on high for 6 to 7 minutes, until cooked, carefully turning the fish half way through cooking.

Garnish with the black olives and lemon wedges. Serve immediately.

Swordfish Steaks with Lemon, Orange and Lime

Serves 4

Working time: about 15 minutes

Total time: about 35 minutes

Calories 250

Protein 30g

Cholesterol 75mg

Total fat 12g

Saturated fat 3g

Sodium 155mg

750 g	swordfish steak (or shark or tuna) trimmed and cut into quarters	**1½ lb**
1	lemon	**1**
1	orange	**1**
1	lime	**1**
1½	tbsp virgin olive oil	**1½**
1 tsp	fresh rosemary, crushed, or ½ tsp dried rosemary	**1 tsp**
1	bayleaf, crushed	**1**
½ tsp	fresh thyme, or ½ tsp dried thyme	**½ tsp**
¼ tsp	fennel seeds	**¼ tsp**
⅛ tsp	cayenne pepper	**⅛ tsp**

Rinse the swordfish steaks under cold water and pat them dry with paper towels. Cut the lemon, orange and lime in half. Cut one half of each fruit into wedges and reserve the wedges for garnish. Squeeze the juice from the other halves into a small bowl. Pour the juices over the fish and let the fish marinate at room temperature for 30 minutes.

While the fish is marinating, pour the oil into a 12.5 cl (4 fl oz) ramekin. Add the rosemary, bay leaf, thyme, fennel seeds and cayenne pepper. Cover the ramekin with plastic film and microwave it on high for 2 minutes. Set the seasoned oil aside until the fish finishes marinating.

Preheat the microwave browning dish on high for the maximum time allowed in the manufacturer's instruction manual. While the dish is heating, brush the seasoned oil on both sides of each swordfish steak. When the dish is ready, set the steaks on it and cook them on high for 90 seconds. Turn the steaks over and cook them for 90 seconds more—they will still be translucent in the centre. Let the steaks stand for 1 minute, then serve them with the fruit wedges.

Editor's Note: If you do not have a microwave browning dish, microwave the steaks in an uncovered baking dish for 5 to 6 minutes.

Shells Stuffed with Crab Meat and Spinach

Serves 6

Working time:
about 30
minutes

Total time:
about 45
minutes

Calories
220
Protein
14g
Cholesterol
50mg
Total fat
8g
Saturated fat
2g
Sodium
365mg

12	giant pasta shells, each about 6 cm (2¼ inches) long	**12**
2 tbsp	safflower oil	**2 tbsp**
1	large onion, chopped	**1**
⅛ tsp	salt	**⅛ tsp**
	freshly ground black pepper	
125 g	fresh spinach, stemmed, washed and sliced into a chiffonade	**4 oz**
2 tbsp	fresh lime juice	**2 tbsp**
1 tbsp	chopped fresh basil	**1 tbsp**

350 g	fresh crab meat, picked over and flaked	**12 oz**
125 g	low-fat ricotta	**4 oz**
	White wine sauce	
12.5 cl	dry white wine	**4 fl oz**
1 tbsp	finely chopped shallot	**1 tbsp**
⅛ tsp	salt	**⅛ tsp**
	freshly ground black pepper	
1 tbsp	chopped fresh basil	**1 tbsp**
1 tbsp	double cream	**1 tbsp**

Preheat the oven to 180°C (350°F or Mark 4). Cook the shells in boiling water with 1 teaspoon of salt, stirring, for 12 minutes—until slightly undercooked. Drain and rinse.

Meanwhile, heat 1 tablespoon of oil in a frying pan. Cook the onion, salt and pepper, until the onion begins to brown—10 minutes. Stir in the spinach, the basil, and 1 tablespoon of lime juice. Cook, stirring, until the spinach wilts—2 minutes.

Remove from the heat. Mix in the crab meat, ricotta, remaining lime juice and more pepper.

Stuff each shell with some crab meat mixture. Put the shells in a baking dish and dribble on the remaining oil. Cover loosely with foil, shiny side down, and bake for 20 minutes.

Put the wine, shallot, salt, pepper and 12.5 cl of water in a saucepan. Bring to the boil, then simmer until only about 6 tablespoons of liquid remain—12 to 15 minutes. Remove from the heat; add the basil, and whisk in the cream. Cook the sauce for 2 to 3 minutes more to thicken it slightly.

Pour the sauce over the shells and serve.

Chops with Aubergine Purée and Vegetables

Serves 4

Working (and total) time: about 45 minutes

Calories 250
Protein 26g
Cholesterol 70mg
Total fat 13g
Saturated fat 3g
Sodium 370mg

4	boned loin chops (125 g/4 oz each), trimmed of fat	4
500 g	aubergines	1 lb
1 tsp	safflower oil	1 tsp
90 g	thick Greek yogurt	3 oz
1 tsp	salt	1 tsp
$\frac{1}{2}$ tsp	ground coriander	$\frac{1}{2}$ tsp
$\frac{1}{4}$ tsp	ground cumin	$\frac{1}{4}$ tsp
4	small fresh mint sprigs	4
	freshly ground black pepper	

Mediterranean vegetables		
2	courgettes, sliced	2
1	sweet red pepper, seeded, deribbed and sliced	1
1	sweet yellow pepper, seeded, deribbed and sliced	1
1	tomato, sliced	1
1 tbsp	safflower oil	1 tbsp
$\frac{1}{2}$	garlic clove, finely chopped	$\frac{1}{2}$
1 tbsp	finely chopped coriander	1 tbsp

Pierce the skin of the aubergines in several places. Brush with $\frac{1}{2}$ teaspoon of oil, place on paper towels and microwave on high for 5 minutes, turning twice.

When cool enough to handle, slice them into 2 cm ($\frac{3}{4}$ inch) thick rounds.

Preheat a browning dish on high for 5 to 7 minutes. Pat the chops dry and brush with the remaining oil. Arrange in the dish with the thickest part to the outside; press down hard. Once the sizzling stops, cook on high for 1 minute, then turn to brown the other side.

Arrange the aubergine slices in the dish, under the chops. Cover and cook on medium for 5 minutes. Leave for 2 minutes, then test the chops with a knife; if the meat is still pink, cook for 1 minute. When fully cooked, remove the chops and keep them warm.

Mix the vegetables with the oil, garlic and coriander. Microwave on high for 3 minutes.

Blend the aubergine, yogurt, salt, ground coriander, cumin and mint. Season with black pepper and serve warm with the chops and vegetables.

Greek Casserole

Serves 4

Working time: about 15 minutes

Total time: about 1 hour

Calories **290**

Protein **23g**

Cholesterol **70mg**

Total fat **8g**

Saturated fat **3g**

Sodium **400 mg**

400 g	lean roasting pork, cut into 2.5 cm (1 inch) cubes	**14 oz**
1 tbsp	potato flour, seasoned with white pepper	**1 tbsp**
1 tsp	virgin olive oil	**1 tsp**
30 cl	unsalted veal stock	**½ pint**
350 g	small (2.5 cm/1 inch) new potatoes,	**12 oz**
4	dried pear halves	**4**

2 tbsp	chunky quince preserve	**2 tbsp**
2 tbsp	honey, preferably Hymettus	**2 tbsp**
4	fresh thyme sprigs	**4**
½	cinnamon stick	**½**
2	5 cm (2 inch) strips lemon rind	**2**
1 tsp	salt	**1 tsp**
4 to 6 tbsp	fresh lemon juice	**4 to 6 tbsp**
	freshly ground black pepper	

Preheat a browning dish in the microwave on high for 5 to 7 minutes. Toss the meat in the seasoned flour. Brush the browning dish with the oil and add the meat. Cook on high for 2 minutes, stirring frequently to brown evenly.

Heat the stock until it is almost boiling. Add 8 cl (3 fl oz) to the meat and cook for 2 minutes on high, scraping the dish with a spatula to detach the brown sediment and thicken the sauce. Add the potatoes, pears, quince preserve, honey, thyme, cinnamon,

lemon rind and retsina, and enough stock to cover the meat. Cook on high until the liquid comes to the boil—10 to 15 minutes. Stir, cover and cook for another 30 to 45 minutes on medium low, until the meat is tender. Stir the contents of the dish once or twice during this time and add more stock if necessary.

Towards the end of the cooking time, add the salt and sufficient lemon juice or more honey to taste. Remove the cinnamon and thyme, season with some pepper and serve.

Frikadeller Pork

Serves 8		
Working (and total) time: about 1 hour		

Calories 112		
Protein 17g		
Cholesterol 62mg		
Total fat 4g		
Saturated fat 3g		
Sodium 206mg		

350g	neck end or other lean pork	**12 oz**
350g	lean veal topside	**12 oz**
1½ tbsp	potato flour	**1½ tbsp**
20cl	soda water, or 1 tsp bicarbonate of soda dissolved in water	**7 fl oz**
1	onion, finely chopped	**1**
1½ tsp	ground caraway seeds	**1½ tsp**

¾ tsp	salt	**¾ tsp**
1½ tbsp	kummel (optional)	**1½ tbsp**
250g	broccoli florets	**8 oz**
250g	cauliflower florets	**8 oz**
250g	small carrots	**8 oz**
250g	kohlrabi or turnips	**8 oz**
1.5 litres	unsalted vegetable stock	**2½ pints**
1	small bunch parsley	**1**

Mince the pork and veal in a food processor until a smooth amalgam is formed. Beat the potato flour and soda water into the meat until the mixture is almost fluffy; mix in the onion, caraway seeds, salt and the kummel. Leave the mixture to chill in the refrigerator.

Cut the vegetables into pieces, about 2.5 cm (1 inch) across. Divide the stock between two cooking pots and bring both to the boil.

To cook the frikadeller, drop teaspoons of the meat mixture into one pot of simmering stock, cooking in batches to allow for expansion. Poach each batch at a gentle simmer for 5 to 7 minutes, turning

occasionally with a slotted spoon. Add more hot water as the cooking stock evaporates. Remove each batch with a slotted spoon and keep warm in a colander placed on the second cooking pot.

While poaching the last batch, cook the vegetables in the second pot of stock. Drain them and reserve the stock.

Once all the frikadeller and vegetables are cooked, combine the cooking liquids and strain through a fine-meshed sieve into a fireproof casserole. Return to simmering point, add the frikadeller and vegetables, warm through and scatter with the chopped parsley. Serve.

Watercress Pork

Serves 4

Working
(and total)
time: about
25 minutes

Calories
195
Protein
25g
Cholesterol
70mg
Total fat
10g
Saturated fat
5g
Sodium
275mg

450 g	pork fillet, trimmed of fat and cut into 7.5 by 1.5 cm (3 by $\frac{3}{4}$ inch) strips	**15 oz**
125 g	watercress, leaves and fine stems	**4 oz**
30 cl	unsalted veal stock	**$\frac{1}{2}$ pint**
1	shallot, finely chopped	**1**
3 tbsp	dry white wine	**3 tbsp**
75 g	fromage frais	**2 $\frac{1}{2}$ oz**
$\frac{1}{4}$ tsp	salt	**$\frac{1}{4}$ tsp**
	freshly ground black pepper	

Reserve some of the watercress for garnish; bring the stock to the boil and blanch the remaining watercress for 1 minute. Drain, reserving the stock, then refresh the watercress under cold running water. Drain the watercress again, then place it on paper towels to dry.

Heat a non-stick frying pan, add the pork and cook briskly for 2 to 3 minutes, turning the strips so they become an even light brown on the outside and are only lightly cooked in the centre. Transfer the strips to a warmed plate using a slotted spoon, and cover to keep warm. Reduce the heat beneath the pan, add the shallot and wine, and cook, stirring occasionally, until the shallots have

softened and the wine has almost completely evaporated—3 to 4 minutes. Add the reserved stock, increase the heat and reduce the liquid until there are only about 3 tablespoons left; add any juice from the meat dish towards the end of the reduction. In a food processor or blender, purée the watercress with the reduced stock. Add the *fromage frais* and purée again. Season with the salt and some pepper.

In a saucepan, reheat the sauce over low heat, stirring; just before serving, add the pork and fold through gently to coat the strips. Serve garnished with the reserved watercress.

Raw Beef Salad

Serves 4

Working time:
about 25
minutes

Total time:
about 1 hour
(includes
chilling)

Calories
120
Protein
12g
Cholesterol
30mg
Total fat
6g
Saturated fat
3g
Sodium
50mg

75 g	young leeks, white and green parts, cut into fine strips about 3 cm (1¼ inches) long	**2½ oz**
175 g	fillet of beef, trimmed of all fat, wrapped in plastic film and chilled in the freezer for 30 minutes	**6 oz**
8	small spinach or rocket leaves,	**8**
4	radishes, trimmed and cut into thin rounds	**4**
¼	cucumber, seeds removed, cut into thin strips with a vegetable peeler	**¼**
75 g	young carrots, cut into fine strips about 3 cm (1¼ inches) long	**2½ oz**
1	lemon, cut into thin wedges	**1**
	Horseradish dressing	
1 tsp	prepared horseradish	**1 tsp**
75 g	thick Greek yogurt	**2½ oz**

First make the dressing. In a small bowl, blend the horseradish into the yogurt. Cover the sauce with plastic film and place it in the refrigerator to chill.

Blanch the leek strips for 10 seconds in boiling water, drain them in a colander and refresh them in cold water. Dry them thoroughly on kitchen paper.

Remove the fillet of beef from the freezer.

Using a long, sharp, flexible knife or a meat slicing machine, cut the fillet into very thin slices. Arrange the meat on four chilled plates.

Assemble the spinach or rocket, the carrots, the blanched leeks, the cucumber and the radishes in separate piles round the sliced beef. Divide the dressing among the plates, and serve the salad immediately with the lemon wedges.

Stir-Fried Ginger Beef with Watercress

Serves 4

Working time:
about 20
minutes

Total time:
about 1 hour
10 minutes

Calories
195
Protein
21g
Cholesterol
55mg
Total fat
7g
Saturated fat
2g
Sodium
440mg

500 g	rumpsteak, trimmed of fat and sliced into thin strips 7.5 cm (3 inches) long	1 lb
½ tbsp	groundnut oil	½ tbsp
1	bunch watercress, trimmed, washed and dried	1
	Ginger marinade	
5 cm	piece fresh ginger root, peeled and finely chopped	2 inch
1 tbsp	chili paste, or 1 tsp hot red pepper flakes	1 tbsp

4 tbsp	dry sherry	4 tbsp
4 tbsp	unsalted chicken stock	4 tbsp
1 tsp	cornflour	1 tsp
1 tsp	sugar	1 tsp
	Cucumber salad	
500 g	cucumbers, seeded and cut into thick strips	1 lb
¼ tsp	salt	¼ tsp
4 tbsp	rice vinegar or distilled white vinegar	4 tbsp
1 tsp	dark sesame oil	1 tsp

Combine all of the marinade ingredients in a bowl. Add the beef and toss it well; cover the bowl and marinate the meat for 1 hour at room temperature.

Combine the cucumbers, salt, vinegar and sesame oil in a bowl. Refrigerate the salad.

When the marinating time is up, drain the beef, reserving the marinade. Heat the oil in a large, non-stick frying pan or a well-seasoned wok over high heat. Add the beef and stir-fry it until it is well browned—about 2 minutes. Add the reserved marinade; stir constantly until the sauce thickens—about 1 minute. Add the watercress and toss the mixture quickly. Serve the stir-fried beef and watercress immediately, accompanied by the chilled cucumber salad.

Beef Braised with Fennel

Serves 4

Working time:
about 15
minutes

Total time:
about 1 hour
15 minutes

Calories
245
Protein
27g
Cholesterol
75mg
Total fat
10g
Saturated fat
3g
Sodium
250mg

600 g	sirloin steak, trimmed of fat and cut into four pieces	¼ lb
¼ tsp	salt	¼ tsp
	freshly ground black pepper	
1 tbsp	safflower oil	1 tbsp
1	large fennel bulb, thinly sliced	1
¼ litre	unsalted brown or chicken stock	8 fl oz
4 tbsp	dry white wine	4 tbsp
1	large carrot, peeled and grated	1
1 tbsp	cornflour, mixed with 2 tbsp of water	1 tbsp

With a meat bat or the flat of a heavy knife, pound the steak pieces to a thickness of 1 cm (½ inch). Season the meat with the salt and some pepper. Heat 1 teaspoon of the oil in a large, non-stick frying pan over medium-high heat and sear the meat on both sides. Transfer the meat to a plate and set it aside.

Heat the remaining oil in the pan and add the fennel. Cook the fennel, stirring occasionally, until it begins to brown—10 to 12 minutes. Return the meat to the pan. Pour in the stock and white wine and, if necessary, enough water to raise the liquid level two thirds up the side of the meat. Bring the liquid to a simmer, cover the pan and braise the meat for 25 minutes. Turn the pieces and continue cooking them for 20 minutes.

Stir the carrot into the pan and cook it for 10 minutes. Whisk the cornflour mixture into the simmering liquid, stir constantly until the sauce thickens slightly. Serve the beef and fennel immediately.

Japanese Simmered Beef

Serves 6

Working time:
about 25
minutes

Total time:
about 40
minutes

Calories
230

Protein
20g

Cholesterol
35mg

Total fat
7g

Saturated fat
2g

Sodium
350mg

500 g	beef fillet, trimmed of fat and thinly sliced against the grain	**1 lb**
125 g	Japanese udon noodles or vermicelli	**4 oz**
1	large carrot, thinly sliced on the diagonal	**1**
60 g	shiitake or other fresh mushrooms, wiped clean, the stems discarded and the caps thinly sliced	**2 oz**
90 g	Chinese cabbage, cut into chiffonade	**3 oz**

3	spring onions, julienned	**3**
250 g	tofu, cut into 2 cm ($\frac{3}{4}$ inch) wide strips	**8 oz**
1.5 litres	unsalted brown or chicken stock	**2 $\frac{1}{2}$ pints**
2 tbsp	low-sodium soy sauce or shoyu	**2 tbsp**
2 tbsp	rice vinegar	**2 tbsp**
1 tsp	finely chopped fresh ginger root	**1 tsp**
1 tsp	finely chopped garlic	**1 tsp**
$\frac{1}{4}$ tsp	dark sesame oil	**$\frac{1}{4}$ tsp**

Cook the noodles or vermicelli in 2 litres ($3\frac{1}{2}$ pints) of boiling water. Begin testing after 8 minutes and cook until they are *al dente*. Drain the noodles in a colander and rinse under running water to keep them separated. Drain again and set aside in a bowl.

Arrange the beef slices, the vegetables and the tofu on a large plate.

Combine the stock, soy sauce, vinegar, ginger and garlic in an electric frying pan,

wok or fondue pot. Bring to a simmer and cook for 5 minutes, then add the sesame oil.

Begin the meal by cooking pieces of the beef briefly in the simmering broth—30 seconds to 1 minute. After the meat has been eaten, cook the vegetables and tofu in the broth just until warmed through—3 to 4 minutes. Finish the meal with the noodles or vermicelli, heating them in the broth. They may be served with or without the broth.

Milanese-Style Braised Veal

Serves 6

Working time: about 40 minutes

Total time: about 2 hours and 45 minutes

Calories 290

Protein 20g

Cholesterol 75mg

Total fat 10g

Saturated fat 3g

Sodium 210mg

600 g	topside of veal, trimmed, cut into 2 cm (¾ inch) pieces	**1 ¼ lb**
2 tbsp	virgin olive oil	**2 tbsp**
3	carrots, coarsely chopped	**3**
2	sticks celery, trimmed and coarsely chopped	**2**
1	onion, finely chopped	**1**
1.25 kg	ripe tomatoes, skinned, seeded and chopped, or 800 g (28 oz) canned plum tomatoes	**2 ½ lb**
2	garlic cloves, one crushed, one chopped	**2**
8 cl	dry white wine	**3 fl oz**
2	bay leaves	**2**
2	strips of lemon rind	**2**
3 tbsp	finely chopped fresh mixed herbs (parsley, oregano, thyme)	**3 tbsp**
¼ tsp	salt	**¼ tsp**
	freshly ground black pepper	
1	lemon, grated rind only	**1**

Heat 1 tablespoon of the oil in a fireproof casserole over high heat, add one third of the veal and brown, turning constantly—5 minutes. Lift out the meat onto a plate lined with paper towels. Repeat with the remaining two batches of veal.

Add the remaining oil to the casserole and lower the heat. Add the carrots, celery and onion, scrape up the sediment from the bottom of the pan, and sweat the vegetables over the lowest heat for 10 minutes. Preheat the oven to 150°C (300°F or Mark 2).

Uncover the casserole and add the crushed garlic, veal, tomatoes, wine, bay leaves, lemon rind, 1 tablespoon of the herbs, the salt and pepper. Bring to the boil, stirring, then cover with foil and a lid. Braise in the oven for 2 hours, or until it is tender. Stir occasionally.

Before serving, mix the chopped garlic, remaining herbs and grated lemon rind. Remove the bay leaves and strips of lemon rind, transfer the contents of the casserole to a warmed serving dish. Sprinkle the garlic, herb and lemon mixture over the top. Serve hot.

Blanquette of Veal

Serves 4

Working time:
about 50
minutes

Total time:
about 2 hours

Calories
190
Protein
20g
Cholesterol
125mg
Total fat
7g
Saturated fat
3g
Sodium
250mg

350 g	topside of veal or top rump, trimmed of fat and cut into 2.5 cm (1 inch) cubes	**12 oz**
8	pearl onions or shallots	**8**
8	button mushrooms, wiped clean	**8**
1	stick celery, cut into chunks	**1**
1	fresh thyme sprig, or ½ tsp dried thyme	**1**
1	bay leaf	**1**
2	parsley sprigs	**2**
60 cl	unsalted veal or chicken stock	**1 pint**
8	small carrots	**8**
1 tbsp	cornflour	**1 tbsp**
¼ litre	semi-skimmed milk	**8 fl oz**
1	egg yolk	**1**
1 tbsp	lemon juice	**1 tbsp**
½ tsp	salt	**½ tsp**
	white pepper	

Put the veal into a heavy, medium-sized saucepan and cover with cold water. Bring to the boil, then drain. Return the veal to the pan and add the onions, mushrooms, celery, thyme, bay leaf, parsley sprigs and stock. Bring to the boil, reduce the heat, cover and simmer for 25 minutes. Add the carrots and simmer for a further 20 minutes. Remove the veal and vegetables with a slotted spoon and set aside. Discard the herbs and strain the stock into a clean pan. Boil to reduce to 30 cl (½ pint)—10 to 15 minutes.

Dissolve the cornflour in a little of the milk. Add the remaining milk to the stock and bring back to the boil. Reduce the heat, whisk in the cornflour mixture and simmer for 10 minutes, stirring. Lightly beat the egg yolk with the lemon juice in a small bowl. Stir in a little of the hot sauce and stir this into the remaining sauce in the pan. Cook gently, stirring, for 1 minute. Add the salt and some white pepper. Return the veal and vegetables to the sauce and heat through gently without boiling. Serve hot.

Grilled Lamb with Chutney Glaze and Mint

Serves 10

Working time: about 30 minutes

Total time: about 1 hour and 15 minutes

Calories 200

Protein 23g

Cholesterol 75mg

Total fat 8g

Saturated fat 3g

Sodium 135mg

2.5 kg	leg of lamb, trimmed of fat and boned	**5 lb**
1 tbsp	safflower oil	**1 tbsp**
¼ tsp	salt	**¼ tsp**
	freshly ground black pepper	
4 tbsp	chopped mint	**4 tbsp**
	mint sprigs, for garnish	

	Chutney glaze	
¼ litre	unsalted brown or chicken stock	**8 fl oz**
4 tbsp	mango chutney	**4 tbsp**
½ tbsp	dry mustard	**½ tbsp**
1 tbsp	cider vinegar	**1 tbsp**
½ tbsp	cornflour, mixed with 1 tbsp water	**½ tbsp**

Spread the boned leg of lamb flat on a work surface with the cut side facing upwards. Remove the membranes and tendons. Starting from the centre of the meat slice horizontally into the flesh at one side of the leg; do not cut completely through the meat. Open out the resulting flap, then slice into the opposite side and open it in the same way. The meat should be no more than 5 cm (2 inches) thick.

Preheat the grill for 10 minutes.

Combine the stock and the chutney in a small saucepan and bring to a simmer over medium heat. Stir the mustard and the cider vinegar into the cornflour paste and then whisk this mixture into the stock and chutney. Cook the glaze, stirring, until it thickens—about 1 minute. Remove from the heat and set the glaze aside.

Rub the lamb with the safflower oil. Grill, turning every 5 minutes, until well browned—about 20 minutes. Sprinkle on the salt and some black pepper on the lamb and brush with some chutney glaze. Cook, turning and basting frequently, for about 10 minutes. Pour the remaining glaze into a small bowl.

Transfer the lamb to a cutting board and sprinkle it with the chopped mint. Leavethe meat for 1 minute before slicing it . Arrange on a warm platter and serve with the remaining chutney glaze and mint garnish.

Leg of Lamb in Spiced Apple Sauce

Serves 12

Working time: about 45 minutes

Total time: about 2 hours and 25 minutes (includes marinating)

Calories 225

Protein 30g

Cholesterol 80mg

Total fat 9g

Saturated fat 4g

Sodium 135mg

2.5 kg	leg of lamb, trimmed and boned	**5 lb**
4 tbsp	cider vinegar	**4 tbsp**
1	onion, finely chopped	**1**
2	garlic cloves, finely chopped	**2**
1 tbsp	finely chopped fresh sage,	**1 tbsp**
½ tsp	salt	**½ tsp**
1 tbsp	freshly ground black pepper	**1 tbsp**
1 tbsp	safflower oil	**1 tbsp**

Spiced apple sauce

300 g	cooking apples, peeled, cored and sliced	**10 oz**
30 g	sugar	**1 oz**
2	cloves	**2**
¼ tsp	ground cinnamon	**¼ tsp**
⅛ tsp	ground allspice	**⅛ tsp**

Cook the apples gently in a heavy-bottomed saucepan with 1 tablespoon of water, until soft and fluffy. Drain off any excess liquid then purée through a nylon sieve. Return the purée to the saucepan, add the sugar and spices, and cook gently, stirring, until reduced to about 12.5 cl (4 fl oz). Remove the cloves and set the sauce aside.

Spread the boned leg of lamb flat on a work surface with the cut side facing upwards. Cut out the membranes and tendons and discard them. Starting from the centre, slice horizontally into the flesh at one side, do not cut completely through the meat.

Open out the flap, then slice into the opposite side and open it out in the same way.

Put the sauce into a large bowl and mix in the vinegar, onion, garlic, sage, salt, pepper and oil. Put the lamb into the bowl and spread the sauce all over it. Leave the lamb to marinate for 1 hour, turning it once.

Preheat the grill for 10 minutes. Remove the lamb from the marinade. Reserve the marinade.

Cook the lamb for 12 minutes each side for medium-rare meat. Baste from time to time with the marinade.

Leave the lamb to rest for 15 minutes, before carving.

Roast Breast of Turkey with Fruit Stuffing

Serves 8

Working time:
about 30
minutes

Total time:
about 1 hour

Calories
255
Protein
23g
Cholesterol
60mg
Total fat
7g
Saturated fat
3g
Sodium
90mg

850 g	boneless turkey breast, with skin	**1¾lb**	
⅛ tsp	salt	**⅛ tsp**	
1 tbsp	safflower oil	**1 tbsp**	
	chopped fresh sage		
	Fruit stuffing		
30 g	unsalted butter	**1 oz**	
6 tbsp	finely chopped onion	**6 tbsp**	
1	large cooking apple, diced	**1**	

1 tsp	sugar	**1 tsp**	
1 tsp	chopped fresh sage	**1 tsp**	
¼ tsp	ground cloves	**¼ tsp**	
125 g	dried apricots, cut into small pieces	**4 oz**	
60 g	seedless raisins	**2 oz**	
3 tbsp	unsalted turkey or chicken stock	**3 tbsp**	
4 tbsp	apple juice	**3 tbsp**	

Sauté the onion in the butter until translucent. Add the apple and sugar and cook until the apple is tender but not mushy—5 minutes. Stir in the sage, cloves, apricots, raisins, stock and apple juice. Simmer, covered, until all liquid is absorbed—5 minutes—stirring once.

Preheat the oven to 180°C (350°F or Mark 4). Put the turkey, skin side down, on a flat surface. Cut a flap in the breast by slicing from the long, thin side towards the thicker side. Do not to cut all the way through. Open the flap and place the turkey between two pieces of plastic film. Pound to an even thickness of about 1 cm (½ inch). Sprinkle with the salt and mound the stuffing in the centre. Wrap the flap round the stuffing and roll the breast into a cylinder with the skin on the outside. Tie securely with string.

Heat the oil in a roasting pan and brown the skin side of the roll. Turn the turkey skin side up and put the pan in the oven. Roast for 20 to 25 minutes, until the juices run clear when the meat is pierced. Remove the turkey from the pan and keep warm.

Serve the turkey sliced thickly, with fresh sage garnish.

Turkey Patties with Beetroot Sauce

Serves 8

Working time:
about 1 hour
and 30
minutes

Total time:
about 1 hour
and 30
minutes

Calories
270
Protein
22g
Cholesterol
45mg
Total fat
9g
Saturated fat
4g
Sodium
440mg

500 g	turkey meat, finely chopped	**1 lb**
1 tbsp	virgin olive oil	**1 tbsp**
125 g	beet greens, finely shredded	**4 oz**
4	garlic cloves, finely chopped	**4**
3	medium potatoes, peeled, boiled, mashed and chilled	**3**
350 g	low-fat ricotta cheese, drained in a strainer for $\frac{1}{2}$ hour	**12 oz**
125 g	spring onions, chopped	**4 oz**
1 tbsp	grainy mustard	**1 tbsp**
4 tbsp	chopped fresh basil	**4 tbsp**
90 g	dry breadcrumbs	**3 oz**

$\frac{1}{2}$ **tsp**	salt	$\frac{1}{2}$ **tsp**
	freshly ground black pepper	
	Beetroot sauce	
10 g	unsalted butter	$\frac{1}{3}$ **oz**
1	medium beetroot, julienned	**1**
$\frac{1}{4}$ **tsp**	salt	$\frac{1}{4}$ **tsp**
$\frac{1}{4}$ **litre**	unsalted turkey stock	**8 fl oz**
1 tbsp	grainy mustard	**1 tbsp**
4 tbsp	sliced spring onions	**4 tbsp**
$\frac{1}{2}$ **tsp**	cornflour, mixed with 1 tbsp cold water	$\frac{1}{2}$ **tsp**

Heat the oil in a sauté pan over medium heat. Add the greens and garlic. Reduce the heat, cover, and wilt the greens for 3 minutes. Stir, and remove from the heat. Allow to cool.

Preheat the oven to 190°C (375°F or Mark 5). Mix together the turkey, mashed potatoes, ricotta, spring onions, mustard, basil, half the breadcrumbs and the cooled greens. Season with the salt and pepper. Form into 16 patties.

Melt the butter in a heavy sauté pan. Add the beetroot and salt and lightly sauté for 5 minutes. Add the stock and cook gently until the sauce is reduced by one third and the beetroot is tender—about 10 minutes. Stir in the mustard, sliced spring onions, and the cornflour-and-water, and simmer to thicken.

Dust the patties with the remaining breadcrumbs. Place on a baking sheet and bake until lightly coloured—15 to 20 minutes. Serve with the sauce.

Turkey Rolled with Ham and Mozzarella

Serves 6

Working time:
about 30
minutes

Total time:
about 40
minutes

Calories
255
Protein
29g
Cholesterol
65mg
Total fat
11g
Saturated fat
4g
Sodium
515mg

8	5 mm ($\frac{1}{4}$ inch) thick turkey escalopes (about 500 g/1 lb), pounded to 3mm ($\frac{1}{8}$ inch) thickness	**8**
125 g	thinly sliced ham	**4 oz**
150 g	low-fat mozzarella, thinly sliced freshly ground black pepper	**5 oz**
3 tbsp	plain low-fat yogurt	**3 tbsp**
30 g	dry breadcrumbs	**1 oz**
1 tbsp	virgin olive oil fresh sage or parsley for garnish	**1 tbsp**

	Tomato sauce with sage	
2	Spring onions, chopped	**2**
4 tbsp	dry white wine	**4 tbsp**
1	medium tomato, skinned, seeded and finely chopped	**1**
1 tbsp	finely chopped fresh sage, 1 tsp dried sage	**1 tbsp**
$\frac{1}{4}$ litre	unsalted turkey or chicken stock	**8 fl oz**
$\frac{1}{8}$ tsp	salt	**$\frac{1}{8}$ tsp**

Preheat the oven to 180°C (350°F or Mark 4). Lay out the turkey slices on a worktop, overlapping them to form a large rectangle. Cover with overlapping ham slices. Place the cheese on the ham; leave a 2 cm ($\frac{3}{4}$ inch) border all round. Sprinkle with the pepper.

Roll the turkey tightly, starting from one of the long sides. Tuck in the ends.

Coat the turkey with the yogurt, then the breadcrumbs. Place in a large, shallow baking dish and dribble the olive oil over it. Bake until firm and springy to the touch—20 minutes. Remove the roll from the oven and let it rest for 5 to 7 minutes.

While the turkey is baking, combine the spring onions and white wine in a small saucepan and reduce to about 2 tablespoons. Add the tomato, sage, stock and salt and simmer for 10 minutes, stirring occasionally.

Cut the turkey into 5 mm ($\frac{1}{4}$ inch) slices. Arrange on a heated serving dish, ladle on the hot sauce and garnish with sage or parsley.

Lentils with Spinach and Carrots

Serves 4

Working time:
about 20 minutes

Total time:
about 50 minutes

Calories
330
Protein
18g
Cholesterol
0mg
Total fat
10g
Saturated fat
1g
Sodium
80mg

250 g	lentils, picked over and rinsed	**8 oz**
1	bay leaf	**1**
2 tbsp	safflower oil	**2 tbsp**
1 tbsp	freshly grated ginger root	**1 tbsp**
250 g	carrots. peeled and cut into batonnets	**8 oz**
12	spring onions, cut into 2.5 cm (1 inch) lengths	**12**
1	garlic clove, crushed	**1**
350 g	spinach, stems discarded, leaves washed, dried and roughly chopped	**12 oz**
2 tbsp	low-sodium soy sauce or shoyu	**2 tbsp**
6 tbsp	dry sherry	**6 tbsp**
1 tbsp	sesame seeds, toasted	**1 tbsp**

Put the lentils in a large, heavy-bottomed saucepan with $\frac{3}{4}$ litre (1 $\frac{1}{4}$ pints) of water. Bring the water to the boil, then reduce the heat to medium, add the bay leaf, cover the pan tightly and simmer the lentils until they are tender—about 40 minutes. Drain the lentils and remove the bay leaf. Rinse the lentils under cold water and drain them again.

Heat the oil in a wok or large, heavy frying pan over high heat. Add the garlic and ginger, and stir them until the garlic sizzles. Add the carrots and spring onions and stir-fry them for 1 minute, then transfer them to a plate. Place the spinach in the pan and stir it over high heat until it begins to wilt—2 to 3 minutes. Return the carrots and spring onions to the pan, add the cooked lentils and stir them for 2 minutes to heat them through. Add the soy sauce and the sherry and bring them to the boil. Stir the ingredients once more, then transfer them to a heated serving dish. Scatter the toasted sesame seeds over the lentils and vegetables, and serve immediately.

Editor's Note: To toast sesame seeds, heat them in a small, heavy frying pan over medium-low heat until they are golden—1 to 2 minutes.

Provençal Casserole

Serves 6

Working time:
about 30
minutes

Total time:
about 3 hours
(including
soaking)

Calories
180
Protein
11g
Cholesterol
0mg
Total fat
3g
Saturated fat
1g
Sodium
90mg

250 g	dried flageolet beans, picked over	**8 oz**
1 tbsp	virgin olive oil	**1 tbsp**
1	large onion, sliced	**1**
1	garlic clove, crushed	**1**
1	sweet red pepper, seeded, deribbed and sliced	**1**
500 g	courgettes, thickly sliced	**1 lb**
1	aubergine, cut into large dice	**1**
15 cl	unsalted vegetable stock	**¼ pint**

500 g	tomatoes, skinned, seeded and roughly chopped, or 300 g (10 oz) canned tomatoes, drained and roughly chopped	**1 lb**
125 g	button mushrooms, wiped clean, stems trimmed	**4 oz**
2 tsp	chopped fresh oregano, or ½ tsp dried oregano	**2 tsp**
	freshly ground black pepper	

Rinse the beans and put them into a large saucepan, well-covered with water. Discard any that float to the surface. Bring to the boil and cook for 2 minutes. Turn off the heat, partially cover, and soak for at least 1 hour.

Rinse the beans, place them in a clean pan, and boil, well-covered with water for 10 minutes. Drain and rinse the beans, wash the pan, then replace the beans, cover with water, boil then simmer, covered, until tender—1 hour. Add hot water to the pan as necessary. Drain and rinse the beans.

Heat the oil in a heavy-bottomed saucepan and cook the onion and garlic gently for a few minutes, until softened but not browned. Add the red pepper, courgettes, aubergine and tomatoes, and cook gently for 1 to 2 minutes, stirring frequently. Reduce the heat to low and add the mushrooms, beans, stock, oregano, black pepper and salt. Mix well, cover, and simmer over low heat, stirring occasionally, for 25 minutes, or until the vegetables are tender. Serve hot.

Mixed Root Vegetables Cooked in Orange Sauce

Serves 4

Working time:
about 30
minutes

Total time:
about 1 hour

Calories
160
Protein
4g
Cholesterol
15mg
Total fat
7g
Saturated fat
4g
Sodium
330mg

30 g	unsalted butter	**1 oz**	**175 g**	kohlrabi, peeled if necessary, cut into 2.5 cm (1 inch) chunks	**6 oz**
1	onion, chopped	**1**	**175 g**	celeriac peeled if necessary, cut into 2.5 cm (1 inch) chunks	**6 oz**
1	garlic clove, crushed	**1**	**175 g**	turnips, trimmed and cut into 2.5 cm (1 inch) chunks	**6 oz**
2 tsp	freshly grated ginger root	**2 tsp**	**30 cl**	fresh orange juice, mixed with 15 cl (¼ pint) water	**½ pint**
1 tsp	coriander seeds, crushed	**1 tsp**	**1**	lemon, coarsely grated rind only	**1**
½ tsp	salt	**½ tsp**	**1**	orange, coarsely grated rind only freshly ground black pepper	**1**
175 g	parsnips, peeled if necessary, cut into 2.5 cm (1 inch) chunks	**6 oz**			
175 g	carrots, peeled if necessary, cut into 2.5 cm (1 inch) chunks	**6 oz**			
175 g	swedes, peeled if necessary, cut into 2.5 cm (1 inch) chunks	**6 oz**			

Melt the butter in a large, heavy-bottomed saucepan or fireproof casserole over medium heat. Add the onion and garlic, and sauté them for 3 to 4 minutes, until the onion is transparent. Mix in the ginger and coriander, and cook the mixture for a further minute, stirring constantly. Add all the root vegetables, and the orange juice and water mixture. Bring the contents of the pan to the boil. Reduce the heat to low, cover the pan and simmer the vegetables for 20 minutes.

Stir in the grated lemon and orange rind, the salt and some freshly ground black pepper. Cover again and simmer the vegetables for another 5 minutes. Finally, to reduce and thicken the orange sauce, remove the lid from the pan and boil the vegetables rapidly for 5 minutes. At the end of this time they should feel just tender when pierced with the tip of a sharp knife. Serve hot.

Linguine with Capers, Black Olives and Tomatoes

Serves 4

Working
(and total)
time: about
35 minutes

Calories
300
Protein
10g
Cholesterol
5mg
Total fat
6g
Saturated fat
1g
Sodium
485mg

250 g	linguine (or spaghetti)	**8 oz**	**6**	black olives, stoned and cut lengthwise into strips	**6**
1	garlic clove, very finely chopped, halved	**1**	**⅛ tsp**	crushed red pepper flakes	**⅛ tsp**
1 tbsp	safflower oil	**1 tbsp**	**¼ tsp**	salt	**¼ tsp**
1.25 kg	ripe tomatoes, skinned, seeded and chopped	**2 ½ lb**	**1 tsp**	chopped fresh oregano, or ½ tsp dried oregano	**1 tsp**
1 tsp	capers, drained and chopped	**1 tsp**	**2 tbsp**	freshly grated pecorino cheese	**2 tbsp**

In a heavy frying pan over medium heat, cook the garlic in the oil for 30 seconds. Add the tomatoes, capers, olives, red pepper flakes and salt. Reduce the heat to low, partially cover the pan and cook the mixture for 20 minutes. Add the oregano and cook for 10 minutes more.

About 10 minutes before the sauce finishes cooking, add the linguine to 3 litres (5 pints) of salted boiling water. Test the linguine after 10 minutes and cook until it is *al dente*. Drain the pasta and add the sauce. Mix well to coat the pasta with the sauce. Sprinkle on the grated cheese before serving.

Vermicelli Salad with Sliced Pork

Serves 6

Working
(and total)
time: about
30 minutes

Calories
205
Protein
9g
Cholesterol
15mg
Total Fat
3g
Saturated fat
1g
Sodium
235mg

250 g	vermicelli (or other long, thin pasta)	**8 oz**
½ tbsp	safflower oil	**½ tbsp**
125 g	pork loin, fat trimmed, meat pounded flat and sliced into thin strips	**4 oz**
2	garlic cloves, finely chopped	**2**
3	carrots, peeled and julienned	**3**
4	sticks celery, trimmed and julienned	**4**
2 tsp	dark sesame oil	**2 tsp**
¼ tsp	salt	**¼ tsp**
	freshly ground black pepper	
6	drops Tabasco sauce	**6**
2 tbsp	rice vinegar	**2 tbsp**
1 tsp	sweet sherry	**1 tsp**

Break the vermicelli into thirds and drop it into 3 litres (5 pints) of boiling water with ½ teaspoon of salt. Start testing the pasta after 5 minutes and continue to cook it until it is *al dente.*

While the pasta is cooking, heat the safflower oil in a wok or a large frying pan over medium-high heat. Stir-fry the pork strips in the oil for 2 minutes. Add the garlic and cook for 30 seconds, stirring constantly to keep it from burning. Add the carrots and

celery, and stir-fry the mixture for 2 minutes more.

Drain the pasta and toss it in a large bowl with the pork and vegetable mixture. Dribble the sesame oil over the pasta, then sprinkle it with the ¼ teaspoon of salt, the black pepper and the Tabasco sauce, and toss thoroughly. Pour the vinegar and sherry over the salad and toss it once more. Serve the salad at room temperature or chilled.

Atlantic Kedgeree

Serves 6

Working time: about 45 minutes

Total time: about 2 hours and 30 minutes (includes cooling)

Calories 280

Protein 23g

Cholesterol 90mg

Total fat 2g

Saturated fat trace

Sodium 170mg

500 g	mussels, scrubbed and debearded	**1 lb**	**½**	sweet orange pepper, sliced	**½**
300 g	long grain rice	**10 oz**	**½**	sweet yellow pepper, sliced	**½**
3	sticks celery, sliced	**3**	**175 g**	peeled cooked prawns	**6 oz**
90 cl	unsalted vegetable stock	**1½ pints**		freshly ground black pepper	
150 g	French beans, trimmed, cut into 2.5 cm (1 inch) lengths	**5 oz**	**2 tbsp**	fresh lemon juice (optional)	**2 tbsp**
350 g	cod fillets	**12 oz**	**1 tbsp**	finely cut chives samphire, for garnish (optional)	**1 tbsp**

Place the mussels in a large bowl. Sharply tap any that are open; if they remain open, discard them. Cover the bowl with plastic film, pulled back at one edge, and microwave the mussels on high for 5 to 6 minutes, stirring after 3 minutes. Leave them to cool, then discard any that remain closed. Remove the mussels from their shells. Strain any cooking liquid through a muslin into a bowl, and set it aside.

Place the rice and celery in a large bowl. Bring the stock to the boil, then add it to the bowl with the reserved mussel-cooking liquid. Cover with plastic film as before, and

cook on high for 10 minutes. Quickly stir in the French beans. Set the rice aside to cool.

Put the cod on a plate, thinner pieces towards the centre, and cover with plastic film pulled back at one edge. Cook on high for 3 to 4 minutes, until the flesh flakes easily. Flake the fish, discarding skin and bones. Set aside to cool.

Meanwhile, place pepper strips in a bowl. Cover and cook the strips on high for 1½ minutes, until tender. Pour away any juices, and leave to cool.

Toss together all the ingredients. Season with some black pepper, and add the lemon juice.

Chilled Beetroot Soup

Serves 6

Working time: about 25 minutes

Total time: about 3 hours and 25 minutes (includes chilling)

Calories 60
Protein 2g
Cholesterol 5mg
Total fat 1g
Saturated fat trace
Sodium 205mg

125 g	tomatoes, quartered	**4 oz**	**2**	bay leaves	**2**
350 g	raw beetroots, peeled and grated	**12 oz**	**90 cl**	unsalted vegetable stock	**1½ pints**
1	carrot, grated	**1**	**175 g**	thick Greek yogurt	**6 oz**
1	onion, grated	**1**	**½ tsp**	salt	**½ tsp**
1	small potato, peeled and grated	**1**		freshly ground black pepper	

Put the tomatoes in a bowl with 3 tablespoons of cold water. Cover the bowl with plastic film, pulled back at one edge, and microwave the tomatoes on high for 3 to 4 minutes, until they are pulpy. Sieve the tomato pulp.

Place the beetroot, carrot, onion and potato in a large bowl. Stir in the sieved tomatoes, the bay leaves and half of the stock. Cover the bowl as before, and cook the soup on high for 25 to 30 minutes, until the vegetables are tender; stir the mixture twice during the cooking time. Remove the bay leaves from the soup, then stir in the remaining stock and leave the soup to cool—30 to 45 minutes.

Ladle a little of the cooled soup into a bowl and stir in the yogurt. When the mixture is smooth, add it to the soup and stir to mix it in evenly. Add the salt and some pepper. Chill the soup for 2 hours, before serving.

Chilled Melon and Cucumber Soup

Serves 6

**Working time
about 20
minutes**

**Total time:
about 4 hours
(includes
chilling)**

**Calories
100
Protein
10g
Cholesterol
10mg
Total fat
3g
Saturated fat
1g
Sodium
60mg**

600 g	ripe Ogen melon, seeded, flesh cut into cubes	**1 ¼ lb**
600 g	cucumbers, peeled, seeded and cut into cubes	**1 ¼ lb**
½ tsp	salt	**½ tsp**
30 g	chopped fresh chervil	**1 oz**
60 cl	unsalted chicken stock	**1 pint**
2 tbsp	double cream	**2 tbsp**
	white pepper	
3	slices white bread (90g/3 oz), crusts removed	**3**
15g	polyunsaturated margarine	**½ oz**

Put the melon and cucumber in a heavy-bottomed saucepan with the salt and half of the chervil. Cover the pan and set it over low heat. Cook the cubes gently for 15 to 20 minutes, until they have softened and the juices are flowing. Add the chicken stock and continue cooking for a further 20 minutes.

Purée the contents of the pan in a blender, then pour the soup into a clean bowl and set it aside to cool. Stir the double cream into the cooled soup, together with some freshly ground white pepper. Cover the bowl and place the soup in the refrigerator for at least 3 hours, to chill it thoroughly.

To make the croutons, preheat the oven to 220°C (425°F or Mark 7). Spread each slice of bread very thinly with the margarine and cut the slices into dice. Put the dice on a baking sheet and cook them in the oven for 15 to 20 minutes, until they are golden, turning them frequently during this time, to ensure that they brown evenly. Allow the croutons to cool on the baking sheet.

To serve, remove the soup from the refrigerator and stir it well. Transfer it to a tureen. Sprinkle the chervil over the surface of the soup and serve the croutons separately, in a small bowl.

Sesame Chicken Breasts with Jellied Beetroot

60 cl	dry white wine	**1 pint**
2 tsp	caster sugar	**2 tsp**
1 tbsp	powdered gelatine	**1 tbsp**
500 g	cooked beetroot, peeled, sliced and cut into long batons	**1 lb**
8	skinned and boned chicken breasts (about 125 g/4 oz each)	**8**
75 g	sesame seeds, toasted	**2½oz**

10	green cardamom pods, seeds only, lightly crushed	**10**
2 tsp	ground cumin	**2 tsp**
1½ tsp	chili powder	**1½ tsp**
½ tsp	salt	**½ tsp**
	freshly ground black pepper	
1	egg white	**1**
8 tsp	soured cream, for garnish	**8 tsp**

Put the wine and sugar in a saucepan, and bring just to the boil. Pour it into a heatproof bowl and sprinkle on the gelatine, whisking well until the gelatine has dissolved. Leave to cool slightly, then stir in the beetroot. Refrigerate it for at least 3 hours, or overnight, until the jelly has set.

Preheat the oven to 180°C (350°F or Mark 4), and lightly grease a baking dish. Wipe the chicken breasts on paper towels. Mix together the sesame seeds, crushed cardamom seeds, cumin, chili powder, salt and some black pepper, and spread this mixture out on a plate. In a small bowl, lightly whisk the egg

white. Dip each chicken breast into the egg white, then coat it in the sesame-seed mixture, pressing the seeds and spices on with the back of a spoon. Place the coated breasts, skinned side up, in the baking dish and bake them for about 25 minutes, until they are just cooked through. (The juices should run clear when a skewer is inserted into the thickest part of a breast.) Set the breasts aside and leave them to cool before slicing.

Serve with the jellied beetroot, and garnish each portion of beetroot with a teaspoon of the soured cream.

Pickled Peppers with Mussels

Serves 4

Working time:
about 25
minutes

Total time:
about 1 hour
and 15 minutes
(includes
chilling)

Calories
100
Protein
14g
Cholesterol
10mg
Total fat
2g
Saturated fat
0g
Sodium
150mg

1	sweet red pepper, seeded, deribbed and thinly sliced	1
1	sweet green pepper, seeded, deribbed and thinly sliced	1
1	sweet yellow pepper, seeded, deribbed and thinly sliced	1
6 tbsp	white wine vinegar	6 tbsp
2	garlic cloves, peeled	2
1 tbsp	demerara sugar	1 tbsp
2 tbsp	chopped parsley	2 tbsp
20	large mussels (500g/1 lb), scrubbed and debearded	20

Place the sliced sweet peppers in a medium-sized saucepan with the garlic, wine vinegar and sugar. Bring the vinegar to the boil, then cover the pan and reduce the heat; simmer the peppers for 7 minutes. Stir in 1 tablespoon of the chopped parsley, and allow the peppers and their liquor to cool.

Put 3 tablespoons of water and the mussels in a large saucepan, cover the pan and bring the water to the boil. Steam the mussels until they open—3 to 4 minutes. Drain the mussels in a colander, discarding the liquid and any mussels that remain closed. Leave the mussels to cool.

Chill the peppers and the mussels in the refrigerator for at least 30 minutes before serving. To serve, divide the peppers among four individual plates, arrange the mussels on the peppers, pour over the pepper liquor and sprinkle the remaining parsley on top.

Burmese Curried Noodles with Scallops and Broccoli

Serves 6

Working
(and total
time) about
35 minutes

Calories
280
Protein
26g
Choiesterol
25mg
Total Fat
9g
Saturated fat
1g
Sodium
440mg

350 g	dried rice-noodle squares	**12 oz**
3 tbsp	safflower oil	**3 tbsp**
1	large onion, chopped	**1**
3 tsp	finely chopped garlic	**3 tsp**
1 tbsp	finely chopped fresh ginger root	**1 tbsp**
1 tsp	ground turmeric	**1 tsp**
½ tsp	ground cumin	**½ tsp**
1 tbsp	ground coriander	**1 tbsp**
350 g	broccoli florets	**12 oz**
1½ tsp	grated orange rind	**1½ tsp**
4 tbsp	fresh orange juice	**4 tbsp**
2 tbsp	fresh lemon juice	**2 tbsp**
½ tsp	salt	**½ tsp**
350 g	scallops, each sliced in half	**12 oz**
4	spring onions, chopped	**4**
250 g	fresh water chestnuts, peeled and sliced	**8 oz**
45 g	thinly sliced shallots, stir-fried in 4 tbsp safflower oil until browned and crisp, drained	**1½ oz**

Heat 1 tablespoon of the oil in a hot wok or a heavy frying pan over medium heat. Add the onion, 1 teaspoon of the garlic, the ginger, turmeric, cumin and coriander. Cook, adding water as needed, until the onion is soft.

Heat 1 tablespoon of the oil in a frying pan over medium heat. Add 1 teaspoon of the garlic and cook it for 30 seconds, stirring. Add the broccoli, cover the pan, and cook the mixture for 3 minutes. Uncover the pan and continue cooking, stirring, until the broccoli is tender—about 1 minute more.

Cook the noodles in boiling water with 2

teaspoons of salt until *al dente*. Drain the noodles, add them to the onion mixture, and toss gently. Add the orange rind, orange juice, lemon juice and salt, and toss thoroughly.

Heat the remaining tablespoon of oil In a wok or frying pan Add the scallops, the remaining teaspoon of garlic, the spring onions and the water chestnuts Stir fry the scallops and vegetables until they are barely done—1 to 2 minutes.

Arrange the dish on a serving platter as illustrated. Garnish with the stir-fry shallots.

Apple Muesli

Serves 6

Working (and total) time: about 10 minutes

Calories 160

Protein 5g

Cholesterol 2mg

Total fat 3g

Saturated fat 0g

Sodium 30mg

1	red apple, quartered, cored and coarsely chopped	1
1	yellow apple, quartered, cored and coarsely chopped	1
12.5 cl	unsweetened apple juice	4 fl oz
75 g	quick-cooking rolled oats	2 ½ oz

1 tbsp	honey	1 tbsp
¼ litre	plain low-fat yogurt	8 fl oz
2 tbsp	sliced almonds	2 tbsp
2 tbsp	raisins	2 tbsp
1 tbsp	dark brown sugar	1 tbsp

Put the chopped apples into a large bowl. Add the apple juice and toss the apples to moisten them. Stir in the oats and honey, then add the yogurt, almonds and raisins. Stir to combine the mixture well.

Serve the muesli in individual bowls; sprinkle each serving with ½ teaspoon of the brown sugar.

Editor's Note: The muesli can be made ahead and kept in the refrigerator, covered with plastic film, for up to two days.

Grapefruit-Apple Compote

Serves 6	
Working time: about 25 minutes	
Total time: about 3 hours (includes chilling)	

Calories
90
Protein
1g
Cholesterol
0mg
Total fat
0g
Saturated fat
0g
Sodium
0mg

3	grapefruits	**3**	
60 g	caster sugar	**2 oz**	

2	sweet green eating apples	2	
4	large plums, halved and stoned	4	

Finely grate the rind of one grapefruit. Squeeze and strain the juice. Put the rind, juice and sugar into a wide, shallow saucepan. Heat gently until the sugar dissolves. Meanwhile, using an apple corer, remove the cores from the apples. Slice the apples into rings about 3 mm ($\frac{1}{8}$ inch) thick. Add the apple rings to the hot grapefruit juice and simmer for about 1 minute, just long enough to soften the fruit slightly. Transfer the apples and juice into a large bowl.

Cut the peel and all the white pith from the remaining two grapefruits. Holding each grapefruit over the bowl containing the apples, segment it, cutting between the connecting tissues.

Slice the plum halves horizontally. Add them to the bowl and mix the fruits very gently together. Cover the bowl and refrigerate for 2 to 3 hours, or overnight.

Orange Slices with Pomegranate Seeds

Serves 6

Working time:
about 15
minutes

Total time:
about 45
minutes
(includes
chilling)

Calories
75
Protein
1g
Cholesterol
0mg
Total fat
1g
Saturated fat
0g
Sodium
3mg

3	oranges	**3**
1 ½ tbsp	finely chopped crystallized ginger	**1 ½ tbsp**
12.5 cl	fresh orange juice	**4 fl oz**
1 tbsp	dark rum	**1 tbsp**

2 tbsp	sugar	**2 tbsp**
½ tsp	pure vanilla extract	**½ tsp**
4 tbsp	fresh pomegranate seeds or one kiwi fruit, peeled, quartered and thinly sliced	**4 tbsp**

Using a sharp, stainless steel knife, cut off both ends of one of the oranges. Stand the orange on end and cut away vertical strips of the peel and pith. Slice the orange into 5 mm (¼ inch) thick rounds. Peel and slice the remaining oranges the same way.

Sprinkle the ginger into the bottom of a 22 cm (9 inch) non-reactive pie plate. Arrange the orange slices in a spiral pattern, overlapping them slightly, and set the pie plate aside.

Combine the orange juice, rum and sugar in a small non-reactive saucepan over medium-high heat and boil the mixture for 5 minutes. Remove the pan from the heat and let the syrup cool slightly, then stir in the vanilla extract. Pour the syrup over the orange slices and chill the fruit thoroughly.

Invert a serving plate over the pie plate, quickly turn both over together, and lift away the pie plate. Sprinkle the orange slices with the pomegranate seeds, or scatter the kiwi fruit over the oranges, and serve at once.

Prunes with Orange, Pineapple and Kiwi Fruit

Serves 6

Working
(and total)
time: about
30 minutes

Calories
90
Protein
1g
Cholesterol
0mg
Total fat
0g
Saturated fat
0g
Sodium
2mg

500 g	dried stoned prunes, quartered	1 lb
1½ tsp	cornflour	1½ tsp
6 tbsp	fresh orange juice	6 tbsp
3 tbsp	honey	3 tbsp
½ tsp	pure vanilla extract	½ tsp

1	orange	1
150 g	fresh pineapple, cut into	5 oz
	2.5 cm (1 inch) wedges	
1	kiwi fruit, halved and cut into	1
	12 pieces (six pieces per half)	

Put the prunes and 60 cl (1 pint) of hot water into a bowl. Cover the bowl and microwave it on high until the water simmers—about 4 minutes. Remove the bowl from the oven and let the prunes stand, covered, for about 10 minutes.

Meanwhile, combine the cornflour and the fresh orange juice in a bowl, then stir in the honey and the vanilla extract. Cook the mixture on high until it thickens—about 2 minutes.

Using a sharp, stainless-steel knife, cut off both ends of the orange. Stand the orange on end and cut away vertical strips of the peel and pith. Slice the orange into 5 mm (¼ inch) thick rounds. Cut the rounds in half.

Drain the prunes and put them into a bowl with the orange, pineapple and kiwi fruit. Pour the honey mixture over the fruits and stir them together gently. Microwave the fruit mixture on high for 1 ½ minutes to heat it through. Serve the fruit warm.

Fresh Fruits in a Watermelon Bowl

Serves 8

Working time:
about 45
minutes

Total time
about 2 hours
(includes
chilling)

Calories
80
Protein
2g
Cholesterol
0mg
Total fat
0g
Saturated fat
0g
Sodium
10mg

1	watermelon (about 3 kg/6 $\frac{1}{2}$ lb)	1
6	ripe figs, washed, stemmed and cut lengthwise into eighths	6
250 g	seedless red grapes, washed and stemmed	8 oz
2	oranges, juice and grated rind	2
1	lemon, grated rind only	1
1 tbsp	ginger syrup, from a jar of preserved stem ginger	1 tbsp
2 tbsp	clear honey	2 tbsp

Slice off the top of the watermelon, about one fifth of the way down. Scoop out the flesh from the lid. Remove the seeds and cut the flesh into 2.5 cm (1 inch) chunks. Reserve the lid.

Run a long-bladed knife round the edge of the large piece of melon, between the flesh and the skin, cutting down deeply and keeping as close as possible to the skin. Make a series of deep parallel cuts, 2.5 cm (1 inch) apart, across the flesh, followed by a series of similar cuts at right angles to the first. Gently scoop out the long, square sections of flesh. Remove the seeds and chop the flesh into cubes. Scrape the remaining flesh from the walls of the watermelon shell, then seed it

and cut it into pieces as before. Reserve the watermelon shell. Put all the pieces of watermelon flesh into a large, heatproof bowl and add the figs and grapes.

In a small, non-reactive pan, mix together the orange juice and rind, the lemon rind, the ginger syrup and the honey. Bring the liquid slowly to the boil and pour it over the fruit. Stir the fruit and syrup together, then leave the syrup to cool for 5 minutes. Stir again, cover the bowl and chill it for 1 hour. Turn the fruit over occasionally, to encourage it to absorb the syrup.

To serve, transfer the chilled fruit to the watermelon shell, replace the lid and stand the whole on a platter.

Exotic Fruit Salad

Serves 12

Working (and total) time: about 40 minutes

Calories 115

Protein 3g

Cholesterol 0mg

Total fat 2g

Saturated fat trace

Sodium 60mg

6	ripe passion fruits	**6**
2	small green-fleshed melons, halved and seeded, flesh scooped into balls with a melon-baller	**2**
1	pink-fleshed melon, halved and seeded, flesh scooped into balls with a melon-baller	**1**
1	pineapple, peeled and cored, flesh cut into chunks	**1**
3	guavas, halved lengthwise, seeded, each half sliced crosswise	**3**
2	pink grapefruits, peeled and segmented	**2**
3	papayas, peeled and seeded, flesh cut into chunks	**3**
2	large mangoes, peeled, flesh cut lengthwise into slices, stones discarded	**2**

Cut the passion fruits in half crosswise. Using a teaspoon, scoop out the seeds and pulp from each passion fruit into a fine nylon sieve set over a bowl. Using the back of the spoon, press all the juice through the sieve into the bowl; discard the seeds and fibrous pulp remaining in the sieve.

Place all the prepared fruits in a large serving bowl and pour the passion fruit juice over them. Gently mix and turn the fruits in the bowl, to ensure that they are all coated with juice. Store the fruit salad in the refrigerator until you are ready to serve it.

Editor's Note: The skin of a ripe passion fruit is very dark in colour and has a wrinkled, shrivelled appearance. Avoid any fruits that have paler, plumper-looking skins; the flesh will taste bitter and acidic.

Papayas and Melon in Sweet Chili Sauce

Serves 8

Working time:
about 30
minutes
(includes
chilling)

Calories
155
Protein
1g
Cholesterol
0mg
Total fat
0g
Saturated fat
0g
Sodium
8mg

1	hot green chili pepper, halved lengthwise and seeded	**1**
12.5 cl	fresh lemon juice	**4 fl oz**

200 g	sugar	**7 oz**
2	papayas	**2**
1	cantaloupe or other melon	**1**

Combine the chili pepper, lemon juice, sugar and $\frac{1}{4}$ litre (8 fl oz) of water in a heavy-bottomed saucepan. Bring the mixture to the boil and cook it until it has reduced to about $\frac{1}{4}$ litre (8 fl oz) of syrup. Remove the chili pepper and set the syrup aside to cool.

Seed and skin the papayas and the melon. Cut the skinned papaya into sticks about 4 cm ($1\frac{1}{2}$ inches) long and 5 mm ($\frac{1}{4}$ inch) square. Cut the melon into 1 cm ($\frac{1}{2}$ inch) cubes. Mix the fruit with the cooled syrup and chill the mixture for at least 1 hour before serving.

Useful weights and measures

Weight Equivalents

Avoirdupois		Metric
1 ounce	=	28.35 grams
1 pound	=	254.6 grams
2.3 pounds	=	1 kilogram

Liquid Measurements

$^1/_4$ pint	=	$1^1/_2$ decilitres
$^1/_2$ pint	=	$^1/_4$ litre
scant 1 pint	=	$^1/_2$ litre
$1^3/_4$ pints	=	1 litre
1 gallon	=	4.5 litres

Liquid Measures

1 pint	= 20 fl oz	= 32 tablespoons
$^1/_2$ pint	= 10 fl oz	= 16 tablespoons
$^1/_4$ pint	= 5 fl oz	= 8 tablespoons
$^1/_8$ pint	= $2^1/_2$ fl oz	= 4 tablespoons
$^1/_{16}$ pint	= $1^1/_4$ fl oz	= 2 tablespoons

Solid Measures

1 oz almonds, ground = $3^3/_4$ level tablespoons

1 oz breadcrumbs fresh = 7 level tablespoons

1 oz butter, lard = 2 level tablespoons

1 oz cheese, grated = $3^1/_2$ level tablespoons

1 oz cocoa = $2^3/_4$ level tablespoons

1 oz desiccated coconut = $4^1/_2$ tablespoons

1 oz cornflour = $2^1/_2$ tablespoons

1 oz custard powder = $2^1/_2$ tablespoons

1 oz curry powder and spices = 5 tablespoons

1 oz flour = 2 level tablespoons

1 oz rice, uncooked = $1^1/_2$ tablespoons

1 oz sugar, caster and granulated = 2 tablespoons

1 oz icing sugar = $2^1/_2$ tablespoons

1 oz yeast, granulated = 1 level tablespoon

American Measures

16 fl oz	=1 American pint
8 fl oz	=1 American standard cup
0.50 fl oz	=1 American tablespoon

(slightly smaller than British Standards Institute tablespoon)

0.16 fl oz	=1 American teaspoon

Australian Cup Measures
(Using the 8-liquid-ounce cup measure)

1 cup flour	4 oz
1 cup sugar (crystal or caster)	8 oz
1 cup icing sugar (free from lumps)	5 oz
1 cup shortening (butter, margarine)	8 oz
1 cup brown sugar (lightly packed)	4 oz
1 cup soft breadcrumbs	2 oz
1 cup dry breadcrumbs	3 oz
1 cup rice (uncooked)	6 oz
1 cup rice (cooked)	5 oz
1 cup mixed fruit	4 oz
1 cup grated cheese	4 oz
1 cup nuts (chopped)	4 oz
1 cup coconut	$2^1/_2$ oz

Australian Spoon Measures

	level tablespoon
1 oz flour	2
1 oz sugar	$1^1/_2$
1 oz icing sugar	2
1 oz shortening	1
1 oz honey	1
1 oz gelatine	2
1 oz cocoa	3
1 oz cornflour	$2^1/_2$
1 oz custard powder	$2^1/_2$

Australian Liquid Measures
(Using 8-liquid-ounce cup)

1 cup liquid	8 oz
$2^1/_2$ cups liquid	20 oz (1 pint)
2 tablespoons liquid	1 oz
1 gill liquid	5 oz ($^1/_4$ pint)